Update...

UPDATE

UNLOCK your happiness
UPDATE differently and
UPGRADE to a light mind

Chet Patel

A catalogue record for this book is available from the British Library.

ISBN: 978-1-9161798-2-0

An Update Differently Project
www.updatedifferently.com

Published, printed and bound by
Outstanding Books
publish@outstandingbooks.co.uk

Cover design by Zain ul-Abedin. Concept by Leila Lal

Typeset by Phil Reynolds Media Services, Leamington Spa

Illustrations Copyright © 2020 Leila Lal

Dedicated to all the light and dark minds that have contributed to this book. Thank you for your inspiration in supporting the development of the mind continuum.

*To Ishver, Bhanu, Hema, Leila and Kecia, with all my love, for believing in my vision to **update** mindsets and support people on their personal journey, their search for happiness; to shine a light on people's minds to lift them out of the darkness and guide them through their own mind continuum... one mind at a time.*

Contents

Unlock your happiness

Y OU SHOULD NOT read this book if you already know the conditions for happiness, if you have no darkness in your life and everything is perfect. If your mindset knows all the answers and you have a clear vision of the destination to which happiness will take you in the future, you are making happy choices or you don't want to challenge your mindset, put this book down and continue watching your Netflix series or scrolling down on your social media. Don't waste your mind. That's the default setting on happiness…

This book is for the mindful people who have realised that the above statement is bullshit, and their current solution is not giving them contentment. This book will help to unlock your happiness and support you on your journey of updating yourself to become light-minded; but it's more about how you can deal with the dark problems of your life better, so increasing the chances that you will be able to search for – and discover – your happiness.

By continuing to read this book, you will have to commit yourself to taking on those dark problems, as happiness never comes from avoiding the suffering and pain that the dark mind creates; the problems never stop, they just change or become amplified. You must search for your own happiness, and it's time to take responsibility and accountability for your conscious mind and ask the questions that will unleash your potential. It's your choice, your mind and your update.

I hope you gift yourself the time for this book, which will help you to unlock your happiness and enjoy developing yourself by updating differently on your terms. This book describes a practical, simple, and proven process that shows you exactly what and how to update to be a better version of yourself. Happiness only occurs when you enjoy dealing with the problems that you find by updating regularly – and those moments make a better you. This process will challenge your mind by making you face up to the difficult questions, but it will be worth it because the outcome will be to change your mind continuum for ever. Just because you can't see it does not mean that it does not exist. The process will increase your vibrations of energy, and help you move out of your comfort zone and align your frequency to your priorities for your personal growth.

I want people to nurture a lighter mindset so they can uplevel their situation to create better conditions for happier outcomes. With a light mind, life becomes an exciting journey with endless opportunities to grow. The ten Updates described in the chapters that follow will shift your mindset and encourage you into actions that will not just help you to grow your mental happiness, but also to accept the struggle for that reward.

This book supports you in your journey to **search** for happiness by updating your mind differently. It's full of tools and strategies that help you focus on your own constant frequency, which in turn creates solutions that allow you to achieve happier outcomes, strengthen your mental well-being and lighten the mind.

● ● ● ● ●

Twenty-five years ago, a young boy in the English Midlands lived in the darkness. In his life he could only see problems, and that made him extremely unhappy and depressed. He could not see any resolutions – as he tried to solve one problem, another one arose – so eventually he just gave up and settled for his problem-driven life.

Every day on his walk to school he suffered racism and abuse, but he just kept walking as there was no way to avoid the bullies, and that made him miserable. During his walks he dreamt about what happiness would look like in the future; but at the same time he became more pissed off as he reflected on how people lived by avoiding their problems, just like himself. He came to know what the rest of us kind of already knew: that suffering totally sucks.

As life got harder and the suffering intensified, something sparked and his mindset switched: maybe happiness comes from **solving** problems? Maybe his pain did have a purpose? He conditioned himself to always look for solutions rather than looking for problems. With experience, he quickly realised that to be happy we need something to solve, and therefore happiness is a form of **action**, not something you buy or pursue.

Placing too much focus on emotional reward fails us, as emotion never lasts – it's just there for a moment. Whatever makes us happy today will no longer make us happy tomorrow because we are preconditioned to need more and are always looking for the next happy fix. An obsession with happiness inevitably amounts to a never-ending pursuit of something else: a larger home, a new car or more holidays. Despite all the hard work and suffering, we end up feeling similar to how we started, locked into the past and left buffering with virus-ridden downloads from our past experiences that do not feel right.

As the years passed, one of his realisations was that life itself is a form of suffering with a list of dark problems. He realised that everyone suffers from these dark problems, and everyone copes with the problems in different ways.

As you may have guessed, that young boy is myself; and I have developed a mind continuum that will support people through their lives in order to achieve optimal physical, mental and emotional development.

●●●●●

We all suffer problems, but how can we create solutions?
- The rich suffer because of entitlement.
- The poor suffer because of poverty.

- People without family suffer because they are lonely.
- People with a family suffer because of their family.
- People who pursue self-image suffer because of it.

This isn't to say that all suffering is equal. Some kinds of suffering are certainly more painful than others. But we will **all** suffer nonetheless.

Happiness is not a solvable equation – for example, *if I do X, that will give me happiness which is Y. If I work really hard to buy that house that will give me happiness*, or *if I work for that promotion that will give me more money to be happier*. Happiness does not work like that. Dissatisfaction and dealing with problems are inherent parts of human nature, and they are elements necessary to create the conditions for happiness.

Through my experiences of connecting with over ten thousand minds from around the world, from the favelas of Rio to the streets of Austin, Texas, I have found that most countries and societies follow a formula for success, which is: *if I work harder, I'll be more successful, and if am more successful, then I'll be happier.* This formula is broken and backward, as every time your mind feels success, you just change the perspective of what success looks like and you want more. You get a good job, but now you want a better job; you just bought a house but you wish it was bigger. We are always updating what success looks like and feels like, and if happiness is on the opposite side of success, your mind never gets there. We have pushed happiness over the cognitive horizon as a society, because we think that we need to be successful before we can be happy.

If you can update in the opposite order then the mind will gain a happiness advantage, which means your mind performs significantly better than the dark mind; you are rewired to create ripples of positivity and happiness.

The reason this book is so important to me is because I was stuck in the darkness for long periods of my life. Having dealt with anxiety, depression, bullying and grief, I was a ZL* for a long time. The list can be endless. Yes, the solution can be found by visiting the health professionals or trying to be positive, but so many of us will not manage it due to lack of self-confidence, or social parameters. Just being positive for a short time is not enough; it has to be a mindset, not a way of thinking.

Living life every day is full of problems and challenges. We suffer for the simple reason that it's biologically useful. It is nature's preferred agent to inspire and nurture change. If you reflect on any tragic world events, such as earthquakes or even terror attacks, they always lead to some sort of change: in legislation, policy, behaviours or mindsets.

● ● ● ● ●

When you think of real success stories, some of the ones that come to mind (time to do some research!) are:
- Rocky: the story behind the story. His story is very inspiring as it is full of suffering and pain but he shifted his mindset.

---

* ZL = Zero Light – see page 11

- Steve Jobs: Stanford commencement speech. His story describes how he discovered happiness at the end of his life.
- Oprah Winfrey: groundbreaking. Her story is about unlocking her mind to keep finding solutions to break barriers.

These are all stories of people that have shared their journeys of hope and happiness.

So many people ***want*** to do something amazing and are made for greatness in their lives, but there are so many that 'stop the light' when it becomes difficult and settle for their own default setting. Success is not determined by what you enjoy, but by how much pain you want to sustain during your life. You can't create the conditions for happiness if you want a pain-free life; you have to love the process of being solution-driven, which is painful and exciting at the same time. You need to search for the frequency that you would like to make consistent.

The process of mind exploration will make you better equipped to manage your mind continuum. The concept is based on the balance between your dark and light thoughts, which do not have a clear dividing point. It's not 'left-wing' or 'right-wing'; like a political opinion, it is a journey along a continuum, continuously changing from light to dark and from dark to light. It differs from your time continuum as that is something no one can control; time is relative and its only purpose is to provide the dividing line between the past, present and future. The reality is ultimately timeless, but your mind continuum is not.

Update One
Incubate the mind continuum

WHAT MAKES YOU *you*? Is it your mind? Your genes? Is it your environment and experiences? Perhaps even your looks?

The question is, whatever it is that makes you *you*, can you affect it or even change it? Your answer to this question gives us a glimpse into your current mindset.

A mindset is simply a belief: a belief about yourself and your most fundamental qualities like ability, intelligence, personality, talents and how you perceive the world.

People with a dark mindset believe that fundamental qualities like intelligence and goals are essentially stable: they don't change over time. People with a light mindset believe that these qualities are growable: they are open to change, and can flourish in certain circumstances and not in others.

Three questions for you to consider before you start the update:

1. Do mindsets matter?
2. Are mindsets changeable?
3. What mindset am I?

If you consider the answers to the first two questions above to be *yes* and *yes*, that is the whole point of this book – mindsets really ***do*** matter.

Let's get real: we're living in an age when most people are lowering their expectations. We live in a time of tremendous uncertainty; a time when large volumes of people in the UK believe that the quality of life for themselves now, and for their children in the future, is far lower than it was in the past. We're in a time of change – where we must update, and not just buffer.

No matter how successful you are, there's a gap between where you are and where you want to be. If your job is going great, you very often don't have time for your family. If your relationship with your children is going well, maybe your body is out of shape or you don't have time for others.

For the past forty years, I have passionately pursued the answers to the questions, 'What influences human behaviour?' and 'How do we develop our mindset and how does it change?' Through the research I've conducted, and my interaction with ten thousand minds from thirty countries, I've developed some fundamental tools and processes to help expand our capacities as human beings and significantly update the pace at which we can achieve our true aspirations and desires. From these interactions, the mind continuum model was born.

In the process, I have also come to realise something about *energy*. The Law of Conservation of Energy states that energy can neither be created nor destroyed; it can only be transferred, or changed from one form to another: from dark to light. The secret is to find your personal frequency and keep the energy moving.

Every update and experience is energy that enters your body, but the mind will light up and create actions and behaviours that differ. The update that creates the biggest energy surge in the western world is *money*; it can make you or break you. How often do we hear stories of very successful actors, and even sportspeople, who become dark-minded when they find it difficult to cope with fame, and the fortune that has been placed upon them?

This book is about unlocking the energy inside you that can help you to break through any limit and create the quality of happiness that you desire and deserve. I'm truly thrilled and fortunate to have this opportunity to share with you the best of what I have learned about personal growth and happiness. This book is not about what *success* is; its sole aim and purpose is to update your mental happiness and create real, happy moments in your life going forward. Life can be exceptional for those who are willing to update their minds in ways that they have never previously considered. Let's make a joint obligation today to participate in this process together, creating a new level of power to learn and update.

Which mindset are you?

During the process of writing this book, I realised that everyone has a certain mindset. In my research I came across a huge number of these, but I found I was able to develop four simple types (ZL, LL, HL and UL) into which all these mindsets could be grouped.

To understand what you need to update if you are to develop a lighter mind, you first need to reflect on which mindset you currently are.

Zero light = ZL

A zero light mindset is when you are **not** updating your life, your mind is filled with dark memories of pain and suffering from the past, and your mental health is poor. You may suffer from symptoms of depression and a disconnect with society, and you may practise self-harm through addictions or substance abuse.

Having no new updates in your life means that your mind stays in the dark, so the chances of you having any hope to change are potentially zero; but there is always hope for some light to penetrate the dark-filled mind.

This mindset is dangerous, not just for that person, but also for all the people around them. When I researched this mindset, it was most evident in people who had become homeless as they wanted to cope with their issues on the dark streets on their own, rather than in the light and with some hope, either in their previous home or a new home. When I connected with people who were self-harming through abuse of substances like alcohol and drugs, they were using these substances to prevent the dark memories from coming to the surface and stopping any chance of light or hope entering.

Low light = LL

 A low light mindset is when some updates and some new experiences are entering your life and your mind, but you have limited processing power to decode the information and create value from the update.

To give you an example, I met a student finishing her final year at university. She talked about all her nights out, and all the people she met during her journey; but she never made a meal for her friends, and never used public transport, as she had anxieties about social connection.

This is a great example of a low light mindset and how the mind limits the updates and the light, prioritising them according to challenge and difficulty. The mind only selects the updates that will be downloaded quickly, choosing the lowest risk option that presents minimal challenge. The low light mindset is always looking for shortcuts, as the mind is programmed to spend minimum effort but to want maximum results – focusing on the outcomes rather than valuing the process.

High light = HL

A high light mindset is when the mind is continuously updating with new experiences and has the processing power to decode the information and create some value from the new update. The important difference between low and high light is that your perspective changes from the *I* game to the *we* game; you start to be mindful of other people's perspective and reflect on how they feel.

Unlimited light = UL

An unlimited light mindset is when the mind is updating with unlimited experiences and has the unlimited processing power to decode the information and create unlimited value to yourself and others around you. The perspective changes from your own to others', and you start to feel how your behaviour and actions affect those around you; you stop thinking about what people are thinking about you and you start thinking about what you can do for them. You become mindful of your actions to unleash your unlimited potential and light up the world, you discover your happy frequency and you consistently shine bright.

You have now selected a starting point for the mindset you currently are, and the mindset you would like to be.

It is now time to update your mind, for the life you deserve; to overcome the buffering holding you back and start living the life you desire. The ten Updates that follow will support you in becoming a lighter mind, helping you to unlock and update the forces inside you to break through your buffering and take control of your mind continuum.

No matter what you want in life – love, passion, happiness, purpose – *uplevel* the mind from within and it will give you the drive and momentum to achieve it. Don't settle for being an LL and live a default life when you can be a UL and live an updated one!

Let's start the Update…

The light minds

The mind continuum concept is developed from research and observations of over ten thousand different minds from around the world: from the drug lords of Rio to the millionaires of Dallas, from the inner-city schoolkids of Leicester to the homeless in Australia. It revolves around the belief that you can rethink a situation to achieve a better outcome or a worse one, in terms of life, intelligence, goals, happiness and the way we think. Life is a like a ray of light full of colourful moments; it's both challenging and supportive, and there is no escaping its fluid movement towards the next light experience or dark moment.

A *mind continuum* is a continuous series of emotions or experiences that vary by such tiny differences that they can't be measured or even felt, but when all the small differences are put together, it creates a huge mind shift or mind swing. It's like a pendulum on a grandfather clock: you control the frequency, you control the swing from right to left and left to right. The frequency is dependent on the volume of updates (learning) you want to achieve: the faster you consistently update your reality, the faster the frequency of your personal growth. The swing to the left is actioning an update to a solution, and the swing to the right is the pain of the process. The process of discovering happiness is the constant frequency of swing from dark to light and light to dark – but the key word is *constant* movement.

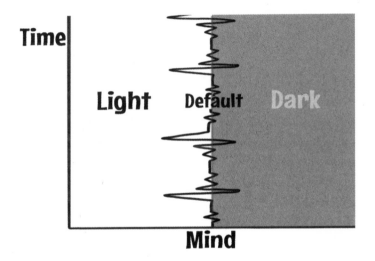

Every person in the world has their own mind continuum, and nobody knows how much time they have; but everyone is accountable for their own development and frequency. The default mind, or average life, is occupied in avoiding both the dark problems and the light solutions and just having limited frequency or energy to your life; the pendulum swings slowly as you are resisting change, or vigorously as you are looking for a quick happy fix. During the development of your mind continuum you will continuously become light- and dark-minded, but the key is being mindful of this and progressing to the next Update constantly and consistently.

Key Update

The process of happiness involves maintaining constant frequency between dark and light. You will have to take on the dark problems of your life, as happiness will never be the outcome if you avoid suffering and pain. Keep swinging from the right to the light, but try not to spend too much time in the darkness.

The mind continuum has five interconnected beliefs:

A light mind unlocks the problem, and actions solutions for happier updates to your *Life*. Your *Intelligence* is continuously being updated, as the brain is malleable and always logged on, adopting a growth mindset to achieve your *Goals* which are limitless. Your *Happiness* is grown from internal value, and is following your own aspirations while being connected to society, and *Thinking* divergently by generating abstract solutions in order to update.

A dark mind locks the problem, and the buffering (over-thinking) process starts. When the problem is amplified, the mind shuts down the emotions. Intelligence (or the learning process) is logged off, and a fixed mindset is adopted. The goals are rigidly defined and have limited scope for deviation. In this mindset, happiness is grown from external value and is following other people's dreams while being disconnected from society. The thinking is very linear and based on logic, rules and rationality.

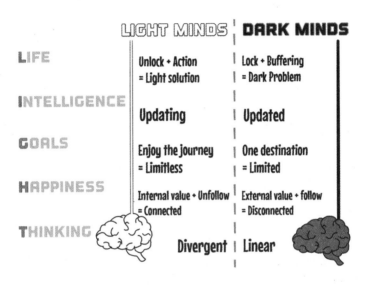

	LIGHT MINDS	DARK MINDS
LIFE	Unlock + Action = Light solution	Lock + Buffering = Dark Problem
INTELLIGENCE	Updating	Updated
GOALS	Enjoy the journey = Limitless	One destination = Limited
HAPPINESS	Internal value + Unfollow = Connected	External value + follow = Disconnected
THINKING	Divergent	Linear

The dark mindset holds to the belief that a person's life is in the dark and cannot be changed, as we are conditioned to think and behave this way. However, years of research has shown that mindsets are malleable. My work shows the power of our most basic beliefs. Whether conscious or subconscious, they strongly affect what we want and whether we succeed in getting it.

Much of what we think we understand of our personality comes from our mindset. This both propels us and prevents us from fulfilling our potential. What are the consequences of thinking that your life is something you can develop and lighten, as opposed to something that is dark and unchangeable?

As you begin to understand the light and dark mindsets, you will see exactly how one thing leads to another – how a belief that your qualities are always in the shadow leads to a host of negative thoughts and actions, and how a belief that your qualities can be cultivated leads to positive thoughts and actions, taking you down an entirely different path.

● ● ● ● ●

What's the best way to start to manage your mind continuum? One way is to identify where you may have dark mindset tendencies so that you can work to become more light-minded. We all live upon a continuum, and consistent reflection helps us become the person we want to be. When we finally allow ourselves to embrace the light, with all its colours of life's rainbow, the highs, the tears, the laughter, then we find the mechanism to manage our continuum.

The mind continuum makes you mindful of your *unconscious mind* which continues to influence your behaviour and experiences. The unconscious can include repressed feelings, hidden memories, habits, thoughts, desires and reactions. Our *conscious mind* contains all the thoughts, memories, feelings and wishes of which we are aware at any given moment. It's time to master your mind continuum, to be mindful of your unconscious mind and make the *unknown, known*.

We often see books with titles like *Ten Habits of the World's Most Successful People* crowding the shelves at Waterstones, and these books may give many useful tips.

But they're usually a list of unconnected habits, like 'Take more risks!' or 'Take a chance on success!' While you're left inspired by the people who can do that, it's never clear how these things can be placed together or how you could ever become that way. So you're inspired for a few days, but basically, the world's most successful people still have their hidden secrets that they don't want to share.

Sure, people with the dark mindset have read the books that say: *success is about being your best self, not about being better than others; failure is an opportunity; effort is the key to success.* But they can't put this into practice because their basic mindset – their belief in their dark traits – is telling them something entirely different: that success is having more than others, that failure is no option, and that effort all leads to one destination.

So let's consider the thought process you must be going through. For you to consider reading or even engaging with this book, you must be asking yourself at least some of the questions below. The questions are in five sections, reflecting the five interconnected beliefs associated with the mind continuum, and will help to start the conversation in your own head about your current mindset and where you want to go with it from here.

Life – What do I want from life?

1. Why am I not happy with my life?
2. There must be more than this?
3. Why do I always overthink?
4. Why do I never action what I think?
5. Why is life full of problems?

Intelligence – Can it be grown?

6. Why do I doubt my own ability?
7. Am I doing the right thing with the knowledge I currently have?
8. Why don't I understand others?
9. Why can I never make a right decision?
10. What do I need to learn?

Goals – What am I looking for?

11. I am successful – why don't I feel it?
12. What do I do now that I have achieved all my goals? (Or: what if I don't even have goals?)
13. Why have I lost my hunger?
14. Why am I limiting myself?
15. What if I want to learn something else?

Happiness – What does it feel like and is it sustainable?

16. Why do I hate the situation I am in?
17. I have everything, so why am I not happy?
18. Why am I lonely and don't feel valued?
19. Why do I paint a perfect life to others when I am not happy inside?
20. Why do I feel disconnected from other people?

Thinking – What's my mindset?

21. How do I start to change?
22. Why don't I know what to do?
23. Why do I always think like this?
24. Why don't I like the way I've been programmed?
25. Why don't I understand the world?

Select one question that you relate to from each area, or create your own question that will update your personal development and growth going forward.

Life _____

Intelligence _____

Goals _____

Happiness _____

Thinking _____

Update Two
Search for your mindset

Dawn and Adrian

I AM INTRODUCING TWO characters that will help you to understand the differences between light-minded and dark-minded people. So let's welcome Dawn and Adrian to the book. It's not really important what gender they are or what they look like – I want you to consider their mindsets and the actions and behaviours they display.

Dawn means the first appearance of light at daybreak, and is comparatively rare. It is sometimes used as a name for Eos, the Greek goddess of the dawn.

Dawn is a light-minded guy who always sees the positive side of life; he plans well and he takes action quickly, and he is used to failing. He is continually learning, and is always trying new experiences as he embraces change. He is always enjoying the journey and has no limits to his aspirations and goals; he knows his priorities and has a clear purpose, which is being himself.

He has high self-esteem and confidence in his own ability, and he makes his decisions independently. He is a social person and cares about his friends and family, and he uses social media for new ideas and to stay connected. He is always choosing an alternative path and is liked for his positive actions. He has a creative mindset, and that is displayed in his daily actions.

He is a very selfless person and he always makes a connection with anyone he meets in a positive light; he is always willing to listen and support others. He is very determined to achieve his own aspirations. Dawn loves cooking and is always experimenting; he mostly eats in but likes to occasionally eat out.

Adrian means dark, just like his mind. Adrian is a dark-minded man who always sees the negative aspects of life. His life is very structured with no flexibility; he likes routine and does not like change.

He overthinks most decisions, so he does not get much done as he wants everything to be perfect. He thinks he knows all the answers and is not willing to try or learn anything new. He is very competitive, and he always wants to win at whatever cost.

He presents himself with high self-image, but lacks self-esteem as he wants reassurance from people around him. He is a social animal and he is always in the crowd on social media, always looking for the greatest number of likes, but he is disconnected in person. He is always following other people's lives and does not really know himself.

He is liked for his external value, but he never really wants to understand other people's feelings and way of thinking. He follows others and spends a lot of time chasing others' dreams. He never thinks outside the box as he is selfish; there is 'I' in his team.

So, I hope you can imagine someone with these habits in your life; now we are going to understand how the five elements of the mind continuum apply to each mindset.

Life: How do we live our life?

Light-minded life is a process where your mind is unlocked, ready to take quick actions and continually learn from life's challenges. The mind sees the light in every opportunity and challenge that is presented; the mindset is resilient and always forward-looking, both in thinking and actions. The light-minded person is solution-driven, always looking for a resolution and anticipating the next problem and its solution; it is a constant cycle of pain and happiness.

Dawn is open to new experiences or challenges; he would rather say *yes, and I will make it happen* first, rather than say *later* or *no*. He does not spend much time thinking, but more time planning and putting into action his thought processes. He is continuously editing his life and is always looking for light solutions to create conditions for happiness.

Dark-minded life is when you are locked into your old beliefs, and the mind buffers (overthinks) when making decisions and when life gets difficult. I know so many unhappy people who are in denial of their problems; or, even worse, people that see themselves as the victim.

Once I knew a woman, we'll call her Amy.

Amy was a businesswoman and, on any given day, if you asked her what she was doing, she would rattle off a number of actions she was involved in and clients she was working with. She dressed to kill every day, but her self-esteem was at rock bottom. She was always buffering when making decisions – not just because she didn't want to make a decision but, more importantly, she didn't want to be seen to make the wrong one. Amy spent so much time talking about how good she was that she forgot to, you know, actually ***do*** something.

Amy is *entitled*. That is, she feels she deserves good things without actually earning them. She believes she should be likeable and well connected without actually helping anyone. Entitled people show a high degree of self-confidence, and this can be alluring to others, at least for a little while; I have to admit chilling with her sometimes made me feel invisible in the room.

But the problem with those who have a sense of entitlement is that their dark mind makes them need to feel good about themselves all the time, even at the expense of those around them. Once the dark mindset has been developed, they are programmed to constantly interpret what happens around them as self-glorifying, and it's hard to rewire this behaviour.

Entitlement closes in upon those who possess it, creating a bubble around them, distorting anything and everything in such a way as to reinforce itself. People who feel entitled view dark problems as a threat to them. If something good happens to them, it's because of some amazing feat they achieved. If something bad happens to them, it's because somebody is jealous and trying to shut them down. People who are entitled fool themselves into whatever feeds their sense of arrogance, but entitlement is a failed solution: it's just another high. It's not happiness.

A real measure of self-worth is how a person feels about positive or negative experiences. A person like Amy hides from her problems by making up success stories at every opportunity. A person who actually has high self-worth is able to look at the negative experiences and find light solutions to grow and improve from that experience. But entitled people become incapable of improving their lives in any meaningful way. They are left chasing high after high, like celebrating every insignificant event and amassing greater and greater levels of denial. But the underlying problems will still be there; it's just a matter of time and how painful the problems will become.

The truth is that there's no such thing as a personal problem, and so there is no such thing as a personal solution. If you have a problem, chances are millions of other people have had the problem in the past, have it now or are going to have it in the future.

Put simply, you're not unique. The realisation that your problem is not special in its seriousness or pain is the first and most important step to unlocking the problem; but for some reason more and more people, especially the millennials, are forgetting this.

The deeper the pain, the more helpless we feel against the dark problem and the more entitlement we adopt to compensate for those problems. The dark mind views the situation in one of three ways:

1. I'm great and the rest of you are all wrong so I deserve special treatment.
2. I'm wrong and the rest of you are great so I deserve special treatment.
3. I'm great and the rest of you are great so we all deserve special treatment.

These dark mindsets often see people flip back and forth between each one, with the person picking the viewpoint that best fits their own selfish demands.

As a retired educator in Leicester with over fourteen years' experience, I saw at first hand a clear correlation between a dramatic decrease in emotional resilience and selfish learner demands in the classroom. When I started teaching, I recognised that my role was as a facilitator of learning; the learners were sufficiently mentally resilient to control their own learning as they valued the process and had a thirst for learning. But for some reason, over time, I found that more students than ever were exhibiting severe signs of emotional distress when it came to everyday school tasks such as improving their work and completing independent research tasks.

It's pretty strange that, in this time when we are more connected than ever, entitlement seems to be at an all-time high. Our insecurities are running wild on social media like never before. The more freedom we're given to express ourselves, the more we want not to have to deal with opposing viewpoints. The easier and more problem-free our lives become, the more we seem to feel entitled for them to get even better.

Intelligence: How do we update ourselves?

Light-minded intelligence is when you are always logged on and willing to update continuously every day, with every new experience being valued. Dawn has adopted a growth mindset where he is always looking to master and improve. Information is continuously being inputted, filtered and sorted to maximise its value.

Dark-mindedness is when you feel you have mastered everything and your mind is logged off when taking in new information and new experiences; you dwell on the past and struggle with new ways of thinking.

Having the internet, Facebook, Instagram and access to limitless amounts of information, there is a tidal wave of positive and negative updates; but our lives today are flooded with information from the extremes of human existence. This has updated us to believe that exceptional is the new average. By definition, most of us are average; but the constant exposure to extreme information drives us to feel insecure and desperate, believing we are not good enough. Once you accept that your average life is worthwhile, only then can you believe yourself to be truly **great**. But a lot of people are afraid to accept mediocrity. This dark mindset is dangerous, since basically it means accepting that 60-70% of people (including yourself) are worthless. So the dark mind will feel more and more the need to compensate through entitlement and addiction. The mind will cope the way it has been conditioned to: by displaying perfect happiness or over-consuming.

Light-minded people are obsessed with continuously updating themselves, and logged on to becoming better by means of small improvements every day. A lighter life involves a growing understanding that you are learning to keep it simple and basic: being kind, helping a friend, cooking a meal for the family, creating solutions, listening to podcasts.

Perhaps that sounds boring, but maybe simplicity is happiness because that is what matters; continuously learning is a key element to happiness.

Goals: What are we aiming for?

Goals help us to focus on what we want to be or where we want to go with our lives. They can be a way of utilising knowledge, and managing time and resources, so that you can focus on making the most of your life potential. By setting goals, you can measure your achievements and keep sight of your progress; if you fail to achieve at one step, you can reassess your situation and try new approaches. Failing and changing your goals is part of the process; success is not incremental and linear.

Light-minded goals are limitless, and the focus is on the journey and the process (which we accept will be painful), unlike the dark mind where the goals are limited and there is only one definition of success. Adrian sees success as only one-dimensional, and his goals are based on other people's expectations. Dawn sees his personal journey as aiming for a balance of a number of goals; but that is the challenge in itself, and it's being mindful of not just achieving your financial goals at the cost of your health goals. Getting this balance right is the key, and will be further discussed in Update Seven.

Setting goals and completing them are two very different things. Don't just think about your goals – write them down physically in your home or workplace. In this way you are creating accountability for, and commitment to, your goals. Think about why you want to make this change. By doing so, you become more aware of what you're dissatisfied with in your life and how you truly want to change it. Write down the details of why it's important, and begin with the end in mind: what will the goal look like once you have achieved it? What will you do once you have achieved it (or not)? Are you willing to change your goals?

Get into the light mindset, no matter how difficult it seems. Be determined to follow through and be willing to fail and experience disappointments on your journey. A limitless thirst to be patient and practical will improve the chances of success; breaking down the goals into small, repetitive tasks will condition you for success.

Happiness: More than a feeling?

Happiness is usually defined in the context of mental or emotional states, including positive or pleasant emotions ranging from contentment to intense joy. The problem – and the solution – is in the definition.

Most people live quite a boring and non-aspiring life on most days; they are hungry for that intense happy fix they get from Friday nights, birthdays, holidays or any other occasion that gives them a reason to celebrate. So let's consider the problem of going big on Friday night to chase the feeling of intense joy, through overconsumption of food, alcohol and other means. This will generate the happy high feeling as it will reduce the feeling of FOMO (fear of missing out); you have a sense of belonging, and the moment grows your self-esteem. For example, we take pictures of our food and post them on social media, a phenomenon affectionately known as 'foodstagramming'. Just as a power station requires gas or coal to power its turbines and generate energy, so **we** need fuel, in the form of food, to power our continued existence. But the fuel that we consume is now used as an excuse to justify our existence on social media.

Every intense happy high will be followed by an extreme low such as less money, poor health, loneliness – or just a banging headache after the night out. So what is the solution? The answer could be 'simple contentment'... What does that mean?

- Become grateful for what you have, never jealous of what you don't have.
- Be in the *we* game rather than the *me* game.
- Become disciplined and break the habit of coping with substance abuse.
- Be yourself and stop comparing yourself to others.
- Be your best friend and be mindful.

Happiness is being mindful of your continuum.

Can it be **that** simple? Not really, as we are programmed to worry about and befriend the unknown; trying to second-guess the future is a common problem. We want to live tomorrow's troubles today, so we hide behind them. We think we can anticipate all possible outcomes but that's where we go off the rails. I like to think that we have enough information with which to make decisions, but sometimes it feels like information fatigue, or a storage overload. And in a situation like this, where the outcome is uncertain, past experiences plus imagination equals anxiety or stress.

Is this overthinking, or does it feel like an Update that has not fully downloaded? You're right to locate the problem in your own hardware, calculate all possibilities, sort them in order of probability. Simulate the experience of the most probable outcomes, so you know what they'll feel like and measure the happiness level when they happen; and also calculate the anxiety level of the next best alternative, to counteract the option we didn't pick.

We are conditioned by default to worry and that creates anxiety. When we were cave people, we had to figure out how to survive and look for food. Our day-to-day concerns have changed, but the worry mechanism hasn't. The one thing we can't change is change itself; everything is in a constant flux.

We live in the most advanced and convenience-led civilisation ever, but so many people don't accept that situation and are still chasing their own fake happiness, which comes from wanting things to be different than they are. We worry our way into the future; relief comes only from staying in the present and choosing the default option, which is the fine life we have.

Light-minded happiness is when you focus on your internal value system, such as self-control and self-confidence; you follow your own aspirations while you are connected with other light and progressive minds. You create your own happiness, and focus on internal conditions to sustain that mindset or feeling. Dawn is unattached to material possessions for happiness, but focuses on creating new experiences and new moments; he accepts that happiness is not something you pursue, but is in the moment you create if the correct conditions are present and updated.

Dark-minded happiness is when you crave external validation though social media, follow other people's dreams and lifestyles and disconnect with progressive minds. Adrian is attached to material possessions that create value and status for himself; he is always scrolling his smartphone searching for that perfect moment or experience that he would like to have. He is always in the *me* game, always looking inwards to how the world and society is affecting him. Selfishly, he is always looking for more, so his happiness will never be created in the present.

Thinking – What do you think?

Light-minded thinking is divergent, so the mind is exploring multiple solutions for the same problem with a growth mindset, whereas the dark mind is looking for the 'right' solution based on logic, rules and a fixed mindset using an old belief system.

Most of us believe we've learned how to think by going to school and learning about the world. But most schooling teaches you only one way of thinking: figuring out the right answer. Once you've done that, many believe that there's no need to reflect on the ideas you have or the beliefs you maintain. But here's the problem with this approach.

In real life, we have to deal with challenges that don't have one right answer; problems with no clear solutions, uncertainties that confuse our brain, behaviour of others that baffles us. I find it enlightening that in our culture we spend so much time and investment on ways to maintain our bodies. Every magazine trumpets the latest discoveries about how to be more physically fit or lose weight. But enhancing your thinking skills? Enriching your mind-management skills? Not many articles about that.

But have you ever heard the saying, 'It's not what you think but how you think it?' Probably not. And yet how you think has a massive effect on how you are in the world.

A light mindset includes reasoning, reflecting, judging, analysing and evaluating an idea or decision. It's using your mind in a creative, effective manner. Thinking tends to be productive, goal-oriented, action-oriented. The dark mind, in contrast, is excessively focused on a single emotion or event. It hinders your ability to relax, let go or decide. This is not merely unproductive, it's **counter**productive.

If you find yourself obsessing, take a moment to reflect and see if you can make one small decision about your problem. It doesn't have to resolve the whole problem, just take one small step. For example, if you are obsessing about whether to leave your job, you might simply decide first of all to contact a headhunter, to get her assessment of what the job market in your field might be before you take the big step and resign.

A light mind will free yourself from the outcome. In previous generations, most people assumed that they couldn't control the outcome of many of life's events. Events occurred, you didn't make them happen. Children 'arrived', they weren't planned. You 'fell in love' (or entered an arranged marriage), you didn't search for the perfect mate. You 'found a job', you didn't agonise over the ideal career. Nowadays, however, because we really do have more control over our lives, we feel anguished when we can't control everything.

If you can free yourself from expecting that the outcome must always be in your favour, you'll make better decisions. Do you want to ask someone out on a date but keep focusing on how you might be rejected? Do you wish to move to a different part of the country but fear that things won't work out as expected? Reflect on your choice. Research your move. Plan your actions. Do what you can to maximise your success. But don't paralyse yourself from taking action just because your success can't be guaranteed.

When I graduated from university with a finance degree and entered the world of accountancy, I quickly realised that I was going to be an average accountant and that was my destination. My mental health was poor, and the buffering was out of control; but I took the action to update my life to become one of the best business teachers in the country, something I would have never imagined in my wildest dreams.

A light mind will cultivate a relaxed mind. It's easy to say 'just relax', but for many that's a really tough thing to do. If you can attain a relaxed state of mind, however, it will help you to avoid obsessive, dark thought patterns. You'll be able to think more clearly and deal more thoughtfully with choices and decisions. A few tips on how to do this:

- Listen to music that soothes your soul.
- Take a warm bath.
- Sit by a fireplace; let yourself be hypnotised by the flames.
- Enjoy something silly.
- Use your imagination.
- Create a place in your mind where you can go to feel safe.

Update Three
Navigate your light

WHY WOULD I WRITE a book to support the growth of others and the community around them, when I am programmed to think only about my own personal development and to work only for financial gain and my own success?

The story begins back in 1979, on January 6th which was when I was first introduced to the world and my life began. I was living in the UK as a first-generation British Indian, but I didn't know what that meant; during my childhood I felt confused and lost.

I was always interested in people and how and why they behaved in the world as they did. My parents both worked in the factories – and they worked extremely hard. I observed that they *only* worked, and didn't really dream or have any of their own aspirations. We were immigrants in a close-knit, white working-class community in Leicester, built up with terraced houses and limited opportunities; people lived day to day, and most people's aspiration was to escape or cope with the day-to-day life. We were in a migrant bubble where all the kids were programmed the same: all made to work hard at school, be educated and not be too white – or be light-minded…

All I believed was that this was home, and I wanted to do better (as I saw it). I felt how hard my parents worked, having gambled to come to England for a better life – not for themselves but for the next generation. I felt a huge responsibility and accountability for that burden; but I questioned if this was a happier life for all.

We didn't have much – the house was always cold and the cupboards were bare – but my sister and I believed that if we got educated, that would be our way out of so-called poverty and we could give ourselves more opportunities and a happier life. Every week was a grind, and it was about surviving and making the most of the limited resources we had; but life was rich with experiences and hard knocks.

Adversity is a gift

My father was very different to the other Asian fathers. He wanted us to learn and update, and he was always compassionate to support that journey; his hands were like sandpaper, and his stare would kill. His mindset was very light; he always made our life difficult, and he made caring and connection his key values, but in a unique way. He never came to my parents' evenings and never watched me play football. I think he believed that this would empower me to develop a growth mindset for my own self-learning and development. Strange but it may have worked.

Being children of migrants living in the Western world, we were programmed to get educated and get a job: accountant, doctor, dentist, pharmacist or lawyer – one of *the* 'big five' jobs that would bring status and wealth, give us a better life and a better reputation in the community, and hopefully make us happy.

We felt constantly insecure as we were always in survival mode. It was extremely difficult for people to see our worth; we would get lost amongst the crowd as we were little fish in a big pond – the insignificant minority who fell through the cracks of society. We were treated as *desi* people: products of the Indian subcontinent who were ill-educated and worthless. Growing up in the eighties was difficult; anything different or coloured was feared, as other people's mindsets were dark.

My sister and I pursued accounting professions at university. She excelled, while I just wandered through the course. I knew I didn't want to continue, but I had to as this was the last year of the government grant system and I wouldn't be able to afford to start a new course.

That is the excuse that I was giving others, but the real reason is that I was not strong enough or confident enough to change direction, as I didn't know what to do. For twenty years of my life I had been programmed to do something that would be the 'right' choice for me; I didn't know whether I would excel in it or have a passion or love for what I did. I was continuously buffering. The feeling was eating me up and my mental health was not in a good place, but I was resilient enough to keep the light mind at the forefront. I was mindful but without actions, which was at least better than having actions and not being mindful.

After graduating from university in 2000, my mind was still buffering. I was torn between getting a job I didn't want or looking for a new update. I took action and bought a round-the-world ticket, deciding to spend the next six months travelling the world. It was the first time I had had the autonomy to decide my own immediate future, with a real goal of developing myself. I felt there were no limits to what I could do on my travels; I would be continuously updating and happiness could be the outcome.

It was an amazing journey over twelve countries in six months. Some memorable Highlights and Updates:

- Capoeira school in Salvador
- Robbed on Copacabana beach
- Beach football in Ipanema
- Forty-hour coach journey to nowhere
- Itaipu Dam
- Real tango club
- Watching my favourite club, Boca Juniors, play
- First five-hundred-dollar car
- Skydive in Picton
- Glacier walk
- White powder sands of Whitsunday
- Top of the red rock
- Big surf

- Jungle bites
- Full moon rave
- Twins of Malaysia
- Singapore Sling
- Marble of love in Delhi.

Success is a journey, not a destination. My experience was amazing; it was a constant update every day with people and cultures that were light-minded. I used every mode of public transport, and every journey and experience was riddled with self-doubt and fear. I quickly observed that every culture and person in the world is searching for happiness, and I was updating with different solutions from the connections I was making every day.

I arrived back in the UK with a lighter mindset, but the world was the same as I had left it six months before. I felt lost and alienated, and so I chose the default function and reprogrammed myself to be the same as others. I continued to apply for accounting jobs with a number of graduate management programmes without any luck. I never questioned my purpose or my core values, but rather tried to be what the corporate world were looking for in the job descriptions. So, I spent a number of months going to interviews and assessment centres, trying to be the person the businesses were looking for, without any luck. I felt worthless and my energy was draining day by day; my dark mind was taking control.

Then my brother-in-law gave me an opportunity to support him in opening a new franchise store in Nottingham. I jumped at the chance as I wanted to prove to myself whether I was capable of success. I enjoyed every minute as I was learning every day and my confidence and self-worth were growing.

With the new sense of confidence and solution-driven mindset, I started again with a new purpose and direction. I took a basic finance job and helped with some football coaching in the local community. I hated everything about the job and knew it was not for me, but I needed time to update to work out a destination for myself.

Update: Are we programmed to play the safe game, the status game – or play the game?

I always wanted to be a footballer as playing football was the only thing I enjoyed and excelled in, but I didn't possess the right mindset at the local trials for Leicester City Football Club and I gave up on my dreams. (Even today I ask the question, how is that we still have *no* British Asian footballers in the Premier League, yet we have representation on game shows, in corner shops and even on *Dragons' Den*?)

So at 24, I chose to unlock my life, action my thinking and update my mind. I was coaching young footballers in the community, and during this experience I realised that I was good at teaching and learning – but more than that, making young people learn and progress quickly. That really made me feel happy ☺. I wanted to nurture that skill I never thought I had. To unlock that potential I needed to get into the classroom and apply my skills in the real world, to change my internal settings.

Update: Network, Network, Network: Connect with friends/family with different professions, mindsets and values. Change your circle, change your mindset

When I looked at the contact list on my phone, I discovered I didn't know one person that was a teacher, a role model I could follow. I questioned my linear thinking and wondered why that was the case?

I realised in my dark mind that everyone in my circle was programmed to aspire to one of the big five jobs; no one wanted to pursue a job in a caring profession with lower pay and long holidays. The only teacher I knew was my former business teacher at my old school (how sad is that 😕). Thank you, Mr Kelly, for unlocking my potential.

So I gave up the terrible accounting job, applied at a local supermarket where a neighbour worked, and my new update began. I worked three days a week as a teaching assistant in the school's business department, as an unpaid volunteer; and three days in the back of the supermarket, taking in deliveries at four in the morning, to pay the bills at home.

My parents were very confused and disappointed by this goal; but they saw me working harder and being happier, so they believed in the process. I had no money at the end of the week and was going to bed exhausted both physically and mentally every night, but it felt right.

It was the first time in my life that I felt alive. I was blinded by the light; I knew what I wanted in my life – to be an exceptional teacher who would help to shape young people's lives. I was growing and updating every day. I applied to every university in the country for a teacher training course. With six months' voluntary experience and a vast amount of business knowledge, I was ready for my next update.

Update: Don't let people interfere with your mindset or vision

I remember the interview day at Nottingham Trent University so clearly. I sat with the other candidates, who were under-prepared and had no real-life skills; everyone in that interview room was straight out of university with no experience in the classroom. The interview went well, my presentation was engaging and learner-focused, and I aced the business test, thanks to the skills I had gained in the real classroom for the past six months. I felt confident about the day and the journey home was positive.

A few days later a letter arrived from the university. It was a rejection. My whole world became dark. I could not see the light, only darkness. All I could see was the third interviewer who hadn't taken a liking to me and made my interview difficult; she closed my door, and she killed my dream.

That particular moment, I felt worthless; as time went on, my feelings remained inside and invisible. I disconnected with the outside world and shut myself down to other people, even my parents. During that period in my life, I was struggling with my mental health; unable to find a positive way to cope, I turned to substance abuse. Alcohol was my dark solution to my problems. I suffered with depression, but I was not mindful of it.

My father felt my pain, and he showed me that it was still possible to have hope; he made me realise that if you continue to do what you are doing, the light will shine again. Option two was a graduate teacher programme that was held in school. I persuaded the school to consider me, and they said yes: all I needed was to pass the interview.

Update: The first step is talking to someone

So, I arrived at the interview with a sense of confidence. I expressed my hunger and drive to get on the course, and shared with the interviewer the story of my disappointment after the rejection by Nottingham Trent. I told him I didn't want to feel that pain again and would rather be told face to face if I had got the place or not.

He smiled and said, 'I think you got this one.' That felt so good walking out of the interview room that day.

Update: Apply to everything as you don't know what you want

During the teacher training programme and whilst attending workshops and observing other teachers in the classroom, I become disengaged with the process as the book theory I was studying was not really relevant to modern-day learners. I was more interested in learners' behaviours in the classroom, how they were learning and how they would update. If I could understand how their minds worked, how they were going to respond and how they would behave, I could enable them to make positive choices and accelerate their learning.

That was when I started my journey to understand the concept of neuro-linguistic programming, or NLP. NLP is simply about understanding how different minds are wired and how that affects the way we behave, so that we can understand ourselves, and others, much better. Being aware that we can all make changes in our thinking and behaviour allows us to take one hundred per cent of the responsibility for the choices we make and to really transform our lives in positive, beneficial ways.

I put this theory into practice by reprogramming myself to look at each situation from three different perspectives. The first perspective is to see it from your own eyes and pay attention to your own thoughts and feelings. The second perspective is to imagine what it is like to be the other person. But the most difficult is the third perspective, which is to imagine being a fly on the wall; what advice would you give yourself about how you are handling the situation? This technique is great to improve your understanding of other people, enable you to think more clearly and provide an opportunity to consider issues objectively.

Update Four
Unlock the mind and declutter

WHAT'S THE FIRST STEP on your journey to update your mind continuum? It's simple: declutter  everything you own. You need to prime the mind before you change the mind. Consider what is important in your life now, and prioritise what will be important in the future for you to grow.

There are three good reasons why this process of *decluttering* is so important for a lighter mind:

1. Practising self-care helps you take control of your home, your life and your 'stuff' to improve your overall well-being. You will be creating an environment that gives you more time and space, and adds energy and clarity to your mindset.

2. A simple life is not seeing how little we can get by with – that's poverty – but how efficiently we can put first things first. When you're clear about your purpose and your priorities, you can painlessly discard whatever does not support these, whether it's clutter in your cabinets or commitments you made on a family WhatsApp group.

3. This process will *eliminate decision fatigue*. Having too much stuff takes so much energy, and not just when it comes to storage. Having to choose which item to use when is exhausting. ***You will now have more time to focus on what's important***. Freedom from the time and energy it takes to deal with a bunch of stuff gives you not only physical breathing space, but mental and emotional breathing space as well.

Simplicity is happiness

There are two areas where you can start the process to declutter: your physical environment and then your mental environment.

It's better to start with your physical environment as you can see the results very quickly and then you can focus on your mental one. Unfortunately, the impulse to buy as much as possible is automatic; we are not able to simply turn it off like a light switch. Hardwired to buy, many of us became poorer, not happier. Once again, our inbuilt impulses have yet to catch up. As a result, many millions of us are filling our homes and lives and suffocating under too much stuff. This problem, which we might call 'stuffocation' (or in my community it could be called 'statusocation'), is the material version of the obesity epidemic. Both obesity and stuffocation are bad for your health. Just as eating too much and being overweight is lousy for your physical health, so having too much stuff and feeling 'stuffocated' is damaging for your mental health.

Physical environment

Our physical environment is where we live and spend most of our time. No two physical objects can occupy the same space at the same time. This is just basic physics. We must choose between a handful of blackberries or a handful of nuts to go into a bowl, because we can't have both occupying the same space. We understand this; we learn it as little kids. We live by it, even if we fight it occasionally (overpacking a suitcase just a bit more?).

In fact, we can even thank this law of physics because it has compelled so many of us to choose a path to a simpler life, to live with less so we can create more space and more openness to breathe and to live a minimalist lifestyle.

We have now chosen to give away the *physical clutter* that piles up in our spaces in exchange for serenity, for simplicity, and for a richer life.

Update: Let's start the process from the top down

Bedroom

- Remove **all** unwanted clothes that don't make you feel great when you wear them. Organise your clothes so you can see them and access them quickly.
- Remove/reduce all superfluous items in your bedroom; you only need **one** of everything (one aftershave, one body cream).
- No gadgets in the bedroom. The bedroom is only for sleeping and relaxing.

Bathroom

- Make everything singular in the bathroom (one of each item).

Kitchen

- Organise your cupboards so you have access to everything easily and efficiently, so you can focus your time on cooking rather than looking for ingredients.
- Try to buy different items that could be used for multiple dishes rather than one dish; keep the items raw and simple. E.g. tinned chopped tomatoes, frozen cod, plain rice, block of cheese, plain oats.
- Only have food you enjoy in your fridge and freezer; consume or give away unwanted items to local food banks.

Living room

- Make the living room the happy room with lots of memories that will inspire you every day. Try to make this room very personal: the place to reflect and light up your life. Don't buy the perfect IKEA living room; make this the space for you to express yourself and where people who visit will know more about you. No fake pictures: make it real.

Garden area

- Make it a place you can enjoy spending time in, and feel proud when you look out on the world.

Car

- Make the car clean and functional.
- Make sure you know how to check the basics in a car such as oil, brake fluid, water and air pressure.

Wallet

- Remove *all* loyalty cards from your wallet – don't be loyal to anything.

Gadgets

- Don't be tempted to have more than one of anything.

Computer

- Organise and create folders for everything so you know its location.
- Delete unwanted files.
- Clean and tidy your emails regularly.

Smartphone

- Remove contacts you don't connect with.
- Remove unwanted apps and pictures.

So, you have removed all the clutter from your physical environment; now to focus on the mental.

Mental environment

What about the non-physical clutter that fills our minds and darkens our vision every day? Why can't we apply the same principle to our thoughts? Unlike physical objects, thoughts can occupy the same space at the same time in our minds. This is usually called confusion, but I call it buffering.

What would we do if we knew for a fact that a positive thought and a negative thought cannot occupy the same space in our mind at the same time? That they cannot co-exist at all? Then we would have to start choosing our thoughts like we choose our clothes for the day.

For a long time, I could not get on board with a growth mindset. It sounded fake and unreal at first. It seemed to make light of my problems; and most of all, it didn't seem to make the situation better. I would scan hundreds of websites and repeat the *positive mindset* over and over to myself. Deep inside, I still felt largely negative, unhappy and far from positive or peaceful.

Worst of all, I felt like a fake. I wanted to be positive. I talked about positivity, and I wanted to believe in it, but it just wasn't working its magic on me and it wasn't for lack of trying. I really did try. My wife can tell you about my sincere attempts, and my Google history can prove how many searches I devoured to prove my interest!

I was committing to the positive thoughts as much as I was holding on to the negative ones. I was thinking, 'I am going to leave my job. I can run a successful business,' as much as I was thinking, 'This is not going to work. I am going to mess it up. It is too late for me to start over.' I repeated and reinforced the good as much as the bad. Since both thoughts could not exist in the same space in my mind, the power of habit sided with the one that it was used to nurturing: the negative thought. It was the familiar voice I knew, and it takes a lot less effort to believe the familiar than to get on board with the new and unfamiliar.

'Out of clutter, find simplicity.' – Albert Einstein

So how do we apply this principle to lighten the mind and remove the clutter for good?

Consider this situation:

You have just upgraded your smartphone, and you have two options. The easier option is to transfer everything from your old phone to your new one, which will mean keeping all your good memories – and your viruses too.

The difficult option is to declutter and filter through your old phone step by step to make sure you only transfer the good memories to your new phone.

Given our love of 'less is more' in the physical world, let's follow a step-by-step approach to clean out the clutter in the mind.

1. **Get ready to replace your smartphone.** Imagine your mind lives in a smartphone filled with stuff: thoughts, worries, anxieties, fears, memories, desires, questions, and more thoughts. Now imagine you are going to replace your smartphone. It has been good to you, no doubt, but the screen is cracked, it feels slower now and you have made the difficult decision to upgrade with a new memory and keep the processing speed to the maximum.

2. **Choose carefully what you reinstall**. You should only download what you want. And only take with you what you plan to use. Ask yourself (with a clear mind and focus): am I going to use the worries, the anxieties, the fears and the negative thoughts? Am I going to use the good memories, the desires and the positive thoughts? Decide on each one as if this were real (because it is). Decide consciously and with intention. What will you choose to take: everything, or just what you need?

3. **Find a space for everything you own on your new smartphone.** Everything needs a space and no two things can occupy the same space at the same time, so it would be best if you brought not quite so much. There's room for only half the stuff in your head anyway!

4. **Live clutter-free now.** If you chose to leave behind the worries, anxieties, fears and negative thoughts, then you have decluttered your mind. You are truly a hero, at minimalism and at developing a lighter mind (and the rest of us envy you!)

But not all of us can detach so quickly from our cosy familiar world, even if that includes our negative thoughts. So if you chose to bring everything – the good, the bad and the dark – your tiny space will be beyond cluttered. That's okay. Just consciously apply the rule: no two things can occupy the same space in your mind at the same time. Choose either a negative thought or a positive one for this day or this hour or this very minute. Discard the other.

For instance, you can either choose a peaceful memory or a big worry, fear or courage, acceptance or denial; and listen, you can choose the worry if you want. Just choose it mindfully. No fooling yourself, and then worry. Worry until you are sick of it. Worry a lot. Then choose fear if you must, and fear as much as you can. Then choose anxiety and be anxious for a few hours. I am not saying you can't choose the bad. I'm just saying you can't choose both, and this is where we finally start to outsmart that clever mind of ours.

It's where you begin to think lighter now. You can have one thought at any given moment, but not two or ten as you start buffering like a smartphone. Sometimes you choose right, sometimes you learn; but if you keep applying the rule, every day you will get closer to the freedom and peace that only a clutter-free mind can give you.

But what if you can't choose? What about the times you feel indecisive, or don't care? That is the first step on the journey of happiness: continuous updating and having no regrets.

Every time you give up the choice, you return to what you know, you go back to the default, to the familiar face, the good old memory. Your familiar default mode is safe, but it's not your full potential. We want to be happy, free of worry and anxiety, free of stress and fear, and definitely free of clutter. We want to fill our minds with positive thoughts and our hearts with peace and joy and love.

So as you settle into your new, minuscule, clutter-free space in your favourite spot in the world which is at home, make room only for positivity, for joy, for calmness, for optimism and for ***happiness***. It's a process, it's an adjustment, it's a new update; it takes time to change, but the mind will start to think differently.

Choose to fill your new mind in this manner, one thought at a time, and you will be surprised how the small stuff adds up to take you where you always belonged: with a quiet, clutter-free, light mind. Consider what you feed your mind and how you update: the music you listen to, the news you watch and the people you surround yourself with.

So now we have primed the mind to let the light in; but we need to understand the origins of the light, and how we could use it to our advantage, for the conditions for mental happiness to flourish.

Update Five
Searching for the light

L IGHT IS INTIMATELY INVOLVED with our daily lives. Many of the unique properties of light are extremely fascinating. Here, we will take one step closer to the wonders of light through its well-known basic properties.

In the world of physics, *light* is a type of energy; it is a form of electromagnetic radiation of a wavelength that can be detected by the human eye. It is a small part of the electromagnetic spectrum which makes up the radiation given off by stars like the sun. Light exists in tiny energy packets called photons. Each colour of light has a specific wavelength or frequency. We are exposed to light every day; from the minute we are born we open our eyes to let the world of light into our lives.

Now let's consider light as a different kind of energy, one that we receive from people around us. Again, we are exposed to this energy every day; we are continuously being charged up like a solar panel with all the light information we receive from the world, both positive and negative; beginning with observations from our parents, and continuing through our schooling, to social media and other sources of memories and experiences, both light and dark.

So, what happens to the light we receive?

Processing the light differently

You cannot create energy by yourself; instead, it enters us from external updates, and can then be converted into actions and behaviours.

However, light behaves in a variety of ways when it comes in contact with us. It can be *absorbed, transmitted through, reflected* or *dispersed*. Everyone has light and dark thoughts inside them, but it's the way we act upon them that counts.

Absorption

When light strikes us, a part of that light is absorbed into us and is transformed into heat energy. We can think of this as a learning process, like riding a bike. We at first find it difficult as we fall over and hurt ourselves a number of times before we learn to balance. The light initially striking us was painful but, through perseverance and dedication, we absorbed the pain and now we can enjoy cycling.

However, this kind of positive absorption is not always the outcome. When I was young I almost drowned in a swimming pool. This dark experience created a negative energy that stopped me from enjoying or trying to learn to swim again. I still have the fear to swim, but it does not stop me from getting in the pool as I control the negative energy and don't let it come to the surface.

Transmission

When light strikes, the light component that was not absorbed within us is *transmitted* through and exits the other side of us. This is the best way to deal with negative light. We are surrounded by people that give us self-doubt or who question what we are doing. The best response is to listen (or take in the light), but not to absorb their energy and turn it into heat. Instead, reflect on the information and just transmit it through your mind and back out into the darkness. Instead of spreading negative noise or dark thoughts into other people's minds, you just transmit the light through your own mind.

To put it another way, you need to not make this a permanent download, just a temporary one, and then delete the thought.

Reflection

Light is reflected in two different ways.

A person whose surface is smooth like a mirror will only reflect light in the same way they have received it. For example, when someone's social media profile expresses a perfect life and the perfect Instagram pose, their self-reflection shows that that is how they want to assess themselves, and they are not willing to change. Adrian fakes the perfect selfie with filters and effects, to display the perfect picture of himself; the ego is programmed to chase the likes and focus on the external value rather than the internal growth. This is when we experience FOMO and compare our dark lives with others around us.

The second type of reflection occurs when the surface is irregular, having pits and protrusions that cause the light to *scatter*. This is real self-reflection as you have the capacity to think about your own feelings and behaviour and the reasons that may lie behind them; you have a deeper understanding of the different rays of light you scatter.

You will understand that you are not perfect and that's okay, and the different rays of light will display all your light and dark-minded thoughts.

Reflection is key for self-development and can be painful as it requires us to question our beliefs and behaviours, but we need to see ourselves in continuous transition and adjustment. Your life and actions are a journey, and success is not a destination.

Dispersion

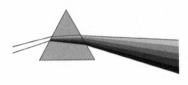

Why do rainbows appear in the sky after it rains? So many people search for that ideal picture and the gold at the end of the rainbow. The light from the sun is called 'white light', but is actually a mixture of different frequencies (colours) of light which appears white to our eyes. In the natural world, water droplets act like a prism when they remain in the air after the rain, causing sunlight to be split up into its component colours. This phenomenon is called *dispersion* of light.

Some people use their own prism or filters to artificially disperse their own light, like trying too hard to show others how great their life is, to create that ideal rainbow. For example, some people spend more than half of their holiday taking and editing photos for their social media instead of soaking in the new surroundings and enjoying the holiday. So how are you going to disperse *your* light? Create a clear white light that you control, or disperse a fake coloured light for everyone to see?

Update: How do others see you?

How do people best describe you? Is it what you do, or what, when, how you behave? WhatsApp three friends this question: how would you describe me in three words?

Reflect on how people see you, and whether you see yourself in the same way.

Light waves

Light travels as a transverse wave, which we can visualise as moving like a roller-coaster, up and down. This motion is similar to the way that, in our lives, we experience huge highs and even greater lows. For example, there are so many mental health issues such as post-natal depression that can follow the great high of giving birth; and parents often feel low after the high of their kids graduating and leaving home – the so-called 'empty nest syndrome'.

There are a number of ways that you could manage your continuum, but basically it boils down to one of two options:

Option 1: Long wavelength with low frequency and low energy

Option 2: Short wavelength with high frequency and high energy.

So let's consider these options. Option 1 is how most people with a dark mind live their lives, the all-too-common phrases being 'living for the weekend' or 'go big Friday'. Adrian has the high of the weekend followed by the low of Monday morning and going back to work (a feeling that we all experience?) and it takes him another four days before he can have that high again. Other than weekends, he only lights up on special occasions such as birthdays and Christmas; the rest of the time he is on a downward spiral, looking back at that one moment of happiness.

In other words, this life will have low-frequency pre-programmed highs, and long time periods with low energy or low moods between these events and occasions.

Option 2 is the light-minded option with short waves, where each day is used to your full potential. Imagine if you programmed yourself to treat every day as Friday. Dawn keeps the momentum going all week; there is no real weekend and he never uses Sunday to relax and do nothing. Living at high frequency means you decide what you would like to do when, rather than basing it on pre-programmed events; for example, I don't buy my kids birthday presents or take my wife out on Valentine's Day – this experience could happen on *any* day. With the high frequency and short distances between events, your personal light energy is amplified and your light mind is free to make your life happy and 'lightful' every day.

Happiness is an energy that can be magnified and intensified on a daily basis. It cannot be created or destroyed; it can only be converted into positive actions. Happiness is a habit or a behaviour that you represent every day. You don't need to *act* happy, you own it because you create it from within through your own actions. The energy you create by living your life on your wavelength and your frequency is limitless as you control the length and frequency of the events in your life. Once you have freed your mind from society and others, you will enjoy the journey to real enlightenment and freedom.

Update: Control your own frequency

The key is to hold your own frequency at all times and be constant. Don't react to the negative influences around you as you will change to other frequencies that are not yours. Having control of your own frequency will empower you to control and discipline your continuum.

Light pressure

Light pressure refers to the fact that, even though individual photons of light are tiny, they nevertheless exert a measurable force on matter. In theory you can move objects by using just light! The average person has seventy thousand thoughts per day; some are positive, but mostly they are negative. So how do we deal with all these dark and light thoughts that are flying towards us, and how much pressure do they exert on us?

On reflection, different people in your life exert different pressures. Someone that you value and respect will create more pressure. Often we can't simply remove ourselves from a dark relationship: maybe with a colleague, an in-law or a parent. When the dark light in our lives drains our energy, it can become a daily challenge to stay positive.

Create or expand your energy so you can cope with the dark minds in your life and reduce the pressure they create. You could choose to disconnect, but you can also choose not to listen. The only pressure that you should experience is your own light pressure to be happy and content with the decisions you take and the actions you make.

Update: Start to cope to create hope

Control your mind, turn the external dark pressure to low and increase the light pressure to high. The pressure can only be controlled by connection or disconnection; you have to control the volume that enters your mind. Connect with light-minded people that inspire you or challenge your thinking to be better, putting positive pressure on you to update to be happier. Increase the pressure by increasing the volume and quantity of the updates, so the light pressure will move your thinking to a higher level and increase its diversity.

The key is updating with a variety of new experiences when choosing food, holidays and activities, for example:

Light mind	*Dark mind*
Go to a network event	Go out for drinks with friends
Try cooking lessons	Eat at your regular restaurant

Paint your own picture	Buy a picture from IKEA
Have coffee with an old/new friend	Have coffee in the car on your own
Talk to someone about finding solutions	Talk to someone about your problems

Disconnect with people that drain you and put dark pressure on you to become logged off and locked into your own fears; the dark pressure is usually based in FOMO, or dark advice from people that fear the light.

When I left the teaching profession three years ago, all my colleagues put dark pressure on my thinking: *what are you going to do, you will lose your pension, how are you going to succeed, what business are you going to start...* In contrast, people with businesses were putting light pressure on my thinking: *there are loads of opportunities for you in the business world, but you just have to find your niche and pursue it.*

Our mind is a tool; like any other tool, it can be used for constructive purposes or for destructive purposes. You can allow your mind to be occupied by dark, unwanted, undesirable and destructive viruses, or you can choose desirable updates like peace, gratitude, compassion, love and joy. Your mind can become your best friend or your worst enemy; someone you can count on to be there and encourage you, or someone that kills every dream you believe in. The choice *is* yours – update differently!

The best strategy is simply not to react to pressure from dark-minded people, as that gives them the confirmation they seek that they have got through to you. Try to create or expand your energy like a force field around you.

You may find thinking of an AAA battery useful to help you remember three important steps in this strategy:

1. Be **A**ware that negative advice or comments come from the person's own insecurities, not yours.
2. **A**ccept that the person really does not understand you or the situation, as their mindset and thinking are different to yours.
3. Now **A**llow them to continue to have that thinking, as you should not waste your energy on people that are not willing to change; use your positive energy for your own growth, and only use your own energy on others wisely.

How can you cope with these pressures?

Light pressure creates an unwanted feeling, much like stress and not being able to cope with life and its struggles. The acronym SCREAM will remind you of the most common causes of poor mental health:

Stressful events – pressures of life
such as work and family

Chronic illness – such as
arthritis, asthma, cancer or
diabetes

Relationship and financial
problems – what relationships
do you have with people and
money?

Emotional problems – depression, anxiety, grief, guilt,
and low self-esteem

Attitudes and perceptions – how you see the world

Mindsets that create buffering – *overthinking* the
situation.

When life is difficult, it's important to be able to *cope*
without feeling emotionally overcome. The solution is to
SCREAM, and connect with people to share how you're
feeling. Another word for this is 'resilience'. In other
words, resilience is the ability to cope with upsetting or
difficult life events.

Coping as a concept isn't defined all that well. Some
definitions refer to the *outcome* of coping: 'He coped well
with that' meaning 'He managed that stressor in a positive
way and the outcome was good.' Some definitions refer to
the *process* of coping and don't consider the outcome at
all: 'She is coping with a lot of concerns at the moment'
meaning 'She is going through a process of managing a
large number of stressors' – but making no reference to
what may happen as a result of that process.

- Be the best and keep updating.
- Deal effectively with difficulties and be able to disconnect from them.
- Become stronger, feel better and move forward.

Most of us manage our physical health far better than our emotional health, allowing issues and problems to cause potential harm. Resilience refers to a person's ability to cope with everyday stress and not suffer undue adverse effects. Having the right coping strategies allows you to 'bounce back' to a mental state that you can control. Often successfully coping with a difficult situation means that you can come back even stronger: *I coped last time, I'll cope next time too.*

A key message is that while life can sometimes throw up difficulties, having a good baseline well-being gives you a cushion that can absorb any stress before it becomes emotionally harmful.

Coping is the ability to manage threatening, challenging or potentially harmful situations and is crucial for well-being. Coping strategies can be either *behavioural* or *cognitive*. Behavioural coping efforts are overt physical or verbal activities, such as exercising and talking, whereas cognitive efforts involve the conscious manipulation of one's thoughts or emotions through disciplines such as mindfulness and yoga.

Update your positive coping mechanism: PADD

Boxers use pads in training to help them learn to keep their hands up, improve coordination, and shift weight during a fight, and these are the exact skills you will need to nurture to win the fight for your mental health. Keep your hands up and take ownership of your own challenge, improve your ability to coordinate your mind and body together to make positive changes, and shift the weight of expectations to *influence* reality and create positive results for yourself.

As individuals, we tend to make decisions based on how others expect us to perform – expectations based on our past behaviours and actions. It's difficult to change, as people are still expecting the old behaviours that created the situation in the first place. As a result, we fulfil those expectations, whether positive or negative, so as to fit in and not create conflict with the situation.

The word expectation comes from the Latin *ex spectare*, literally meaning 'to look out for'. Look out for a change or a behaviour that shows signs that you are actively coping with the situation and believing that something is going to happen, a move in the right direction towards a better you. These 'increments of change' are the small steps to a lighter and brighter you that will cope with your emotions differently.

PADD

PADD is a useful acronym to help you start the process of reflecting on your mental health and coping with the dark. There are four typical ways that people cope with difficult situations; PADD will help you to remember these and to reflect on what ways you fight with your own emotions.

Passive – Deflect to others
Active – Deal with it on your own
Denial – Avoid the situation
Delay – Delay the situation

Passive coping is when you talk to others and discuss possible solutions for your mental health problems. This is a good start as you are talking about your emotions and feelings, but you are not taking responsibility for your own actions as you want others to change or to show compassion for your feelings.

Active coping is the best way to manage your situation as you are taking full accountability for your actions and you are focused on controlling your emotions and looking for solutions for the situation.

Denial is a common coping strategy as people always see the source of the problem in others or just don't accept that the problem is there. It's like a relationship that has become a little sterile, where the couple sleep in separate beds and spend no time together; they may continue to be happy, but they are in complete denial of the situation.

The final strategy is **D**elay; that is, postponing any other coping strategies that could be used currently.

Let's look at the difference between passive and active coping in a little more detail.

Passive coping is when a person feels that they are helpless to deal with the stressor, relying on others to resolve the stressful event or situation. 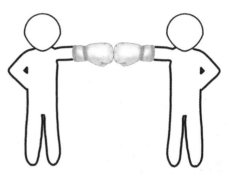 They thus relinquish their control of the stressful situation (and their reaction to it) to others, or allow other areas of their lives to be adversely affected by the stressful event or situation.

You witness passive coping when your best friend tells you everything wrong with their life and you are made to listen, or your social media only highlights the failings with the world and what is wrong with everyone else. The passive coper feels the world and society are falling apart and they are helpless to do anything about it.

Think of this situation. You have just lost your smartphone on the way to work and you believe you are now helpless to do anything; you are relying on others to resolve your situation. You don't have the number for your network provider. How are you going to get a replacement? How are you going to communicate until you do? This problem will adversely affect your mood, and how you function, for the rest of the day. You have limited or no mental resilience to deal with this situation on your own and you are looking for external resolution. In this way, you make yourself vulnerable to the external environment and don't really take control or accountability. This dependence on external help is in contrast to active coping, in which the individual relies upon their own resources to resolve the situation.

I often see a great example of passive coping when I talk to dark-minded people with depression. The first thing they do is go to the doctor for the solution, in the belief that antidepressants will make them feel better and solve all their problems, rather than look at *why* they are feeling depressed and what has triggered these emotions.

Active coping is characterised by solving problems, seeking inform-ation, changing environments, planning activities, and reframing the meanings of problems for yourself. Active coping is thought to be an adaptive way of dealing with stressful events and having control of your own mind; this is a vital component of nurturing self-resilience in the face of stress, health problems, and other adversity. You are proactive in creating or controlling a situation rather than just responding to it after it has happened. This strategy involves dealing with matters and being accountable to yourself to find your own solutions to your problems; in doing so, you are actively seeking to shift your emotions.

How do you FEEL?

The main types of active coping strategies are *emotion-focused* and *solution-focused*, which are both based on how you FEEL.

The simple four-step FEEL strategy will support you on your journey of actively coping with the pressures of life:

Feelings and perception
Environment
Experiences
Learning

Feelings and perception

Your *feelings* about a situation are the things that you think and *feel* about it, or your perspective towards it. When you refer to someone's *feelings*, you are talking about the things that might embarrass, offend, or upset them. Perspective is defined as an attitude towards something, or a way of regarding something. You can't change the things that happen to you, but you can change how you look at things, how you react to things and the impact you allow them to have on your life.

The key to successful coping lies in being able to take a different perspective – to look at things from a point of view other than our own. Changing perspective brings in the mindfulness of compassion and empathy in our relationships and how we see and interact with others. Being *emotion-focused* is maintaining a light perspective and nurturing optimism; the situation doesn't change, but your perception of it does. So what is the difference between a light and a dark perspective? Understanding this is the key to judging how good, bad or important something is in comparison with other aspects of your life.

Let's consider the comic-book villain 'The Joker'. He pushes his arch-enemy to his limits, exploiting his weaknesses in any way he can. The Joker does what he does simply because he likes it; although he's incredibly destructive, he does all of it for 'fun', for the simple reason that it gives him pleasure when others are in pain. His morals are not permanent, as his values and perceptions can change according to what will bring the best outcome for himself.

In the same way, when you have a dark perspective the dark mind will rush to get what you want/need and crave. You lose any kind of external perspective of your life and become selfish. Like a supervillain, you believe yourself to be invincible; you want to have everything your way – whether that means world domination or just to have full control of your situation. You feel that you can continue to behave in the same way as you don't really care about other people and their perspective. The ultimate *me* game, you only consider what is in your own interests and you only see things from the perspective that will benefit yourself. It's the same when people self-harm, or in extreme situations consider suicide; they only see their own perspective.

The supervillain's arch-enemy is, of course, the super-hero. Their personality is defined by a sense of justice, and a willingness to fight for what they see as right. Without their staunch sense of morality, superheroes could easily be villains, using their powers for evil or for selfish gains. Instead, they fight against petty thieves and supervillains alike. Maybe they're just smart, realising that destroying the world is a pretty useless plan in the long run; or maybe they really are guided by a strong sense of right and wrong.

Tweaking your morality takes a bit of self-reflection, but it's totally worth the effort to be light-minded. Reflecting on your core values and considering whether you are still living by them is a valuable exercise. So many dark-minded people have no real values as they are too busy chasing happiness, just as they chase money and the likes on social media.

Update: keep things in perspective and don't buffer on one incident. Move forward.

The reason why so many people struggle with this is because it means taking accountability. It is so, so easy to sit in a cubicle or an office, or even somewhere you enjoy being, and say, 'This place isn't giving me enough. It's not making me grow.' This is the same as blaming other people for how you feel, or your personal issues. Just like a mirror, if you point, your reflection will point back. The key is to point at yourself. If you look in the mirror and you point at your physical self, your reflection in the mirror will point at itself.

When you 'pull your thumb out of your ****,' you take accountability. You are shifting your perspective from *blame* to *ownership*. You are allowing yourself to open up and see opportunity instead of oppression. This same theory goes for everything: work, personal relationships, even the way you feel about yourself.

Environment (internal and external)

This is the second step in the FEEL strategy and focuses on the relationship between you and everything around you. Your *external environment* encompasses not only your natural surroundings but also social settings (such as work and family), built environments, learning environments and informational environments. We'll come to those in a moment.

But first of all let's consider *yourself* – your *internal environment* – and how you feel about *you*; how you deal with your emotions, such as fear, anger, love, jealousy, guilt or anxiety, and how you connect with others around you in a positive way. You need to update and download your own internal resilience and coping strategies so that they are strong enough to cope with any pressures that the external environment creates. Do you deal with life in a positive light mind or a dark negative mind? Are you okay with *yourself* – and what do we mean by that concept?

Self-confidence is one's ability to judge your own social and personal self-worth with respect to your environment and be able to derive satisfaction out of it. This will create the feeling of contentment, that you have some sort of control over your internal environment and don't need to enhance it with external inputs like substance abuse and status. Your self-worth is not found in others; it's found in your internal environment that you create and control.

The *natural environment* is based on where you were born and where you were brought up. Are you a product of your upbringing or your environment? Just because everyone in your area was a drug dealer, does that mean you have to become a self-fulfilling prophecy? I am a product of a deprived and tough inner-city upbringing that taught me to be resilient, have a sense of community and be caring for others; but I now live in a little leafy suburb. I always reflect on the challenge of ensuring that my kids develop these same attributes while growing up in a very different environment.

Your *built environment* is man-made; it's the connections you make with your family, with your friends and work colleagues. The built environment should be ever-changing; light minds search for new communities to update with, while dark minds disconnect with environments that they can't accept or belong to.

Some of these built environments can help sustain your personal growth, but others could really damage it. Consider being in a family environment that always picks the easy options in life. Living with no challenges has its advantages: it's safe, predictable, and generally the default option. Will this environment limit your opportunities to grow and come out of your comfort zone? I don't know about you, but I want to build a life of adventure and positivity that will unlock my potential. In this way you create the feeling of hope that you can cope with the difficult challenges ahead. At the other extreme, your family environment could be full of substance abuse and domestic violence; that may hinder your growth, but even in that environment you are capable of changing or adapting yourself to cope.

Ask yourself the question: why is it that more than 98% of society are seeking to be happy? It means that we have created the conditions for society to grow and evolve, but not to create the basic element of happiness. We have built an environment that seeks wealth and status, and neither of these generates happiness.

According to many of the theorists of happiness today (mainly in Harvard University which has an entire department dedicated to the 'science of happiness'), happiness is the mix between *pleasure* and *purpose*. That is, if you have a lot of purpose in life but little pleasure then you are not happy – and the reverse is also true. In work it is exactly the same. If you find a job that you love doing and which also fulfils your personal expectations, you are very lucky and are more likely to be happy. But many recent studies tell us that, even though nobody talks about it, there is a third key component: *environment*.

If you are a company accountant who has to add and subtract numbers all day long, you may find your job boring; and if you're doing it while locked away in a basement with no natural light, you'll end up with a bullet in the head. There are jobs in which changing your purpose and pleasure is very complicated. But you **can** change the environment. If you put that same person in a pleasant space with natural light and colour, you are changing their environment; and the environment is a factor influencing happiness.

If you look at the world's leading tech companies like Google and Facebook, their employees benefit from perks such as free food, free time, free transport, and their offices are typically equipped with beanbags, sleeping pods, fully stocked kitchens and all kinds of things whose sole purpose is to create an environment where creativity and happiness can flourish. If your environment is not creating happiness and making you feel low, change the environment – that could be your home, workplace or wherever you feel happy.

Experience

As a fanatical Liverpool football fan, I saw my team lose because the young full back was ball-watching and left his man unmarked; the ball went over his head to the attacker, who therefore had time to control it, pick his spot and put it past the goalkeeper. Nevertheless, I stayed quite calm. Having had the experience of losing innumerable times, I am finally able to accept that losing isn't the end of the world! So I didn't react and shout at the TV, as I may have done not so long ago.

However, my calmness was brief on this occasion and only lasted until the expert pundit in the commentary box excused the young full back's actions as being due to a lack of experience! To my mind, the full back's error was just that: the *error* of not applying a fundamental aspect of football defence. Based on the realistic assumption that most children start playing football at about the age of seven, the 19-year-old full back would have had approximately twelve years' experience in the game. How many years do you need before the pundits no longer assign errors to 'lack of experience'?

So that got me wondering: what do we mean by *experience*? A dictionary definition is: 'knowledge or practical wisdom gained from what one has observed, encountered or undergone'. The Latin origins of the word are 'knowledge gained by repeated trials', 'to test, try', and 'feel, undergo'. So, experience is about learning by doing; the emphasis is on practical applications, and involves feelings and sensations.

In this definition we can also glimpse the dark side of the experience 'coin'. What is the actual experience needed to acquire the skill and knowledge to fulfil happiness? One person's experience will be different to another's based on the fact that individuals perceive differently. Experience is about practically acquiring skill and knowledge; but one will only gain that skill and knowledge if there is a dark, negative side to the experience, as people learn more from their losses than their gains. This requires us to develop a level of mental resilience.

For example, if you are an MOT tester and you spend twelve months performing inspections but never come across a defect, is that sufficient experience? Experience counts for very little when you have not encountered a failure that you can accept and use to your advantage in future decision-making and updates. If the experience lacks feedback, or the individual learns incorrect lessons, then it can lead to bad habits, poor skills and misplaced confidence in the experience.

As a facilitator of learning for over fourteen years, I saw my failing students gaining more in the classroom than the successful ones. I continually used to print out and share poor answers; by analysing the mistakes and finding solutions, the students gained more from the experience than if I had simply given them an A* answer to look at.

It is human nature that we learn more from our failures, so fail early and fail hard (and learn to keep failing); but the question is, what is your perspective of the failures, which I call 'learnings'? If you don't learn from failing, the pain of the failure was not dark enough; coming out of the darkness is happiness. We can easily forgive a child who is afraid of the dark; the real tragedy of life is when adults are afraid of the light.

As another example, think of two different approaches to travelling around the world. Adrian always flies first class, stays in the best hotels, travels by private taxi, eats at the finest restaurants and only books all-inclusive resorts when he relaxes. In contrast, Dawn only travels by public transport; he stays in self-catering apartments, eats in local restaurants and never books inclusive or exclusive resorts. So reflect on who is gaining the most from the experience of their travel adventures? Who is going to get lost and stumble across a great restaurant; who is going to meet a local and share a drink; who is going to experience the memorable moments, both light and dark, that will last a lifetime?

An experience is something that you do or that happens to you, especially something important that affects or changes your mindset; people grow through light and dark experiences. If you are choosing to experience dark thoughts and being overwhelmed by past experiences, the only way to change that is to overpower the mind with new positive experiences that will shape and challenge your current mindset.

Life is full of unexpected twists and turns. The moment you think that everything is going smoothly, something changes and all your planning and preparation is wasted. There are times when you think that the whole world is working against you and you are left to deal with it alone. Yes, these experiences are very bad and sometimes even tragic. However, everyone has bad experiences, and that is what makes you tough enough to make it through the uncertainties in life.

Life is a problem, and the challenge is to keep updating your solutions continuously. The key difference is how that experience is viewed and felt. At various times I have experienced all the SCREAM elements listed previously, but I have programmed myself to view each one not as something that will define me, but as part of the process of continually updating myself with new light experiences.

You still have to update

Hanging on to the dark experiences in life is not going to help you in any way, because ultimately it is not going to be your first or your last. So just 'swipe' and take it as a moment instead of getting stuck to it; you have to keep scrolling and find a new update or download. A dark experience is a little like a virus on your phone; it's going to make it slow down and create glitches that will affect its usability. So the only way to get the phone to function well, like your mind, is to find a new update that will get you working efficiently again.

Life is not just about one update. You have a whole lifespan that comprises many decades. As days go by, you will experience changes in your attitude, in your perception and the way you look at things. That is why it is better to keep updating, so the past is left behind and you can look forward with hope and a little curiosity as to what waits for you in the future.

Update: manage the virus

I would not say it is easy, but there is a rule of thumb to help you get over dark experiences. It needs lots of courage and an attitude that is positive towards everything in life. People with a light attitude go a lot further than the dark-minded people, or those who are hesitant about every new opportunity. The way you think always shows in your actions. The things you do in a light frame of mind will succeed, because you approach them in the right way and do not have second thoughts. Light thoughts help you take a new look at the dark experiences that have happened in the past, and they are what allows you to move forward and make a light update.

Since my father passed away seven years ago, I have always been searching for new ways to support people with grief and understand the process of grieving. I met many people that were suffering from grief, and my key learning was that the dark minds saw their current situation as a buffer that was stopping them from moving forward in their life. They shut down their emotions, and felt guilty for enjoying events such as Christmas and birthdays. The light-minded people embraced every event and moment, as they were living more than one life: they were living the dreams of the person who had passed and making every future moment count.

Update: Buffering on the dark experiences

There are dark experiences in life, but there are light experiences as well. It is up to you to decide whether you want to hang on to the good ones or the bad ones. Things that make you smile when you remember the good experiences will give you much-needed confidence and help you grow. However, the dark experiences in life will never let you grow if you buffer or overthink on them.

Dark experiences teach you that everything is not perfect in life. There are glitches and spam in your way, and you have to delete them so you can fully update a lighter experience. So why not clear the dark experiences in life and learn to grow from them?

'Why me?' is something that will encourage self-pity and will not let you grow. You have to take the pain with you and be willing to keep updating. Place the spam in a delete folder, and keep discovering the right updates to remove the glitches.

Learning

The fourth and final step in the FEEL strategy is *learning*. This is your first exposure to the things you know – or you might not. We learn things by seeing, listening or reading; through advice and education; from the experiences of others, and from our bad experiences too. Learning is a continuous process and we should be updating to be the best version of ourselves every day.

Just because you are struggling, that doesn't mean you're not learning. Every failure has something to teach you, and everything you learn helps you grow. If you are unwilling to learn, no one can help you; if you are determined to learn, no one can stop you. Every great success requires some kind of struggle, and good things really do come to those who work smart and strive to pursue the goals and dreams they believe in. To radically change your life, you have to change yourself. Start updating to your new mindset today; keep shifting and updating your thoughts, and that will help you move forward towards your chosen path of happiness and contentment.

As a retired teacher I regularly reflect on the education system I was a part of, which I truly loved. Although it tries to give learners a huge amount of knowledge and understanding, it isn't connected to happiness and personal growth. Because success is praised over effort and commitment, the system programs learners to be dark-minded. Nothing that we have created as a society helps us to be happier.

Solution-focused learning happens when, even though there's nothing you can do to change a situation, you find an opportunity to take action and actually change the circumstances you face. These types of solution-focused learning strategies can be very effective for stress relief; often a small change is all that's required to make a huge shift in how you feel. For one thing, one change can lead to another, creating a chain reaction of positive change; opportunities are opened up, and life can change significantly. Also, once the first action is taken, no matter how small, the sense of being trapped with no options – a sure recipe for stress – can dissipate quickly. It's important to be mindful about which actions to take, as each situation may call for a unique solution, but a less-stressed mind can more easily choose the most beneficial course of action.

Imagine you just bought a new phone. Before you even take it out of the box you purchase a screen protector, a case, a power pack… You are already visualising possible problems in the future, as you care about the smartphone and you want to keep it in good working order; it's of no value to you if it's broken or dead. If this is you, then you are active in your decision-making and problem-solving, always seeking more information to gain clarity and transparency, adapting to changing environments, planning activities for personal updates and self-reflection, and reframing the meanings of problems for yourself continuously.

These strategies are great to use in many situations where you have little ability to control what happens, and you need to see your stressors as a challenge instead of a threat, or change the way you respond to your circumstances in order to diffuse some of the stress involved. Focusing on the lesson, not the problem, will help you to keep updating your mind and moving forward.

● ● ● ● ●

So we have considered the main types of light-minded coping strategies. Let's now consider inactive, dark strategies which are based on being DEAF and disconnected and not being able to ask for help.

DEAF will make you reflect on the journey of inactive, dark tendencies that we experience with the pressures of life:

Depression
Emotions without control
Anxiety and addiction
Fear and failing

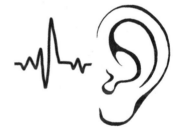

Depression

Depression is having dark thoughts such as self-doubt, and buffering with your decision-making; it has a negative effect on how you feel, the way you think and how you behave. Through my interactions with dark-minded and depressed people I've witnessed a vast range of behaviours: from people having low mood and a loss of interest in life, to people living crazily and immersing themselves in substance abuse like excessive food or drugs.

The feeling is like going into a black hole; you want to cry and scream and kick and shout, but you don't as you shut down your emotions. Either your emotions fall into the dark and you repress your feelings, or you get blinded by the light and amplify that you are feeling amazing.

One of the best things you can do is to update your *concepts* of emotions. Since our emotions are constructed by our mind, we can program the mind to label them more precisely. Some people will simply express that they are 'feeling great' or 'feeling sad', but this is a very simplistic distinction. *Emotionally enlightened* people differentiate more finely between emotions, allowing them to create predictions and construct instances of emotion that are finely tailored to fit each specific situation.

Think of your light or dark feelings as lying somewhere on this vertical scale:

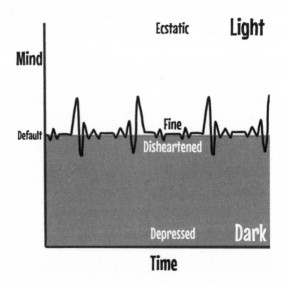

If you can distinguish ten dark shades of sadness (from 'disheartened' to 'depressed') and ten light shades of happiness (from 'fine' to 'ecstatic'), this process of emotional enlightenment will allow you to reframe the situation, leaving you better equipped to scale your emotions and choose the appropriate action in social situations. You will be able to update your emotions, starting the process of feeling happier and moving away from the darker mind.

Emotion without control

Emotion is a mental state brought on by chemical changes in the nervous system and variously associated with thoughts, feelings, behavioural responses, and a degree of pleasure or displeasure. When you can't manage your own emotions, they will control you and take control of your life and your mind.

Ignoring your sadness or pretending you don't feel pain won't make those emotions go away. In fact, unaddressed emotional wounds are likely to get worse over time. And there's a good chance hiding your feelings will cause you to turn to unhealthy coping skills, like food, drugs or alcohol.

It's important to acknowledge your feelings while also accepting that your emotions don't have to control you. Before you can change how you feel, you need to acknowledge what you're experiencing right now. Are you nervous? Do you feel disappointed? Are you sad? Put a name on your emotions. Keep in mind you might feel a whole bunch of emotions at once: like anxious, frustrated, and impatient. Labelling how you feel can take a lot of the sting out of the emotion. It can also help you take careful note of how those feelings are likely to affect your decisions. Your emotions affect the way you perceive events; reframe your thoughts to develop a more realistic view.

If you catch yourself thinking, 'A networking event is going to be a complete waste of time. No one is going to talk to me and I'm going to look like an idiot,' remind yourself, 'It's up to me to get something out of the event. I'll introduce myself to new people and show interest in learning about them.' Sometimes, the easiest way to gain a different perspective is to take a step back and ask yourself, 'What would I say to a friend who had this problem?' Answering that question will take some of the emotion out of the equation so you can think more rationally.

If you find yourself buffering on dark thoughts, you may need to update your mind to see things differently. If you find yourself in a dark mood, you're likely to engage in activities that keep you in that state of mind. Isolating yourself, mindlessly scrolling through your phone, or complaining to people around you are just a few of the typical bad-mood behaviours you might indulge in; but those things will keep you buffering. Take positive action. Think of the things you do when you feel happy; do those things when you're in a bad mood and you'll start to feel better.

Here are a few mood-boosting updates:
- Call a friend to talk about something pleasant.
- Go for a run or walk.
- Listen to some inspiring music.
- Meet a friend for coffee and talk about the future.

Coping with your emotions is tricky at times; and there is likely to be a specific emotion, like fear, that sometimes gets the best of you. But the more time and attention you spend on updating your emotions, the mentally stronger you'll become. You'll gain confidence in your ability to handle dark moods, while knowing you can make healthy choices that shift your mindset and lighten your mood.

Anxiety and addiction

Anxiety is a natural feeling associated with experiencing the unknown, or sometimes an unnatural feeling related to the desire to experience perfection. People who can update and reframe anxiety as excitement and growth can show positive effects and improve performance in their lives. A sympathetic nervous system will create the jittery butterflies and the feeling of sickness but with fewer of the proinflammatory cytokines that lower performance and generally make people feel bad.

Adrian is going for a job interview and feels that his heart is racing and he is sweating more; this could be signs of harmful anxiety. Meanwhile Dawn is sitting opposite him feeling the same emotions, but he has reframed the situation into an opportunity and is feeling energised and ready to go. He has made his butterflies fly in arrow formation with clear focus and purpose. He is saying, 'Yes, you feel stressed, but don't perceive it as nervousness; reframe it as determination and an opportunity to change.' Anxiety cannot be really reduced, but **can** be reframed and redirected.

Addiction is the condition of being physically and mentally dependent on a particular substance or activity that creates dark or light actions and behaviours. Some of the better-known activities that can lead to addiction include work, exercise, video games, and gambling; all depend on a behaviour rather than taking substances. That's because addiction lives in the reward centres of the brain, not in the drug or process. The drug or action just leads the brain to where it wants to go.

Even though our society rewards long working hours and high performance, many of us know the dangers of work addiction, or *workaholism*. If you are working insane hours, have a need to work, and have lost control of your ability to regulate your work life, you are probably a workaholic. If you don't have the compulsion, and hate your job, but are still working insane hours with no real control over the amount you work, you're just buffering.

All work requires sacrifices, so the definition of harm here is a little greyish, but the point is that work is a good thing until it starts to consistently hurt you. At that time, if you still have a compulsion to work, it's an addiction.

Adrian works so much, and so obsessively, that his entire life is preoccupied with his work. His family are neglected, and he gives them little to no time. He rationalises this by telling himself he is making money to provide his family with a good life; but, in exchange, he is sacrificing being present in their lives at all. His addiction tells him this is a worthy trade-off. When he's not at work, he's buffering about it. It becomes an endless game that he needs to win at all costs. Over time, he loses traction on his physical health, his relationships, and his hobbies. All areas of his life suffer as a result. His results at work may be positive, but the rest of his life suffers. It's like the relief an alcoholic or heroin addict experiences when taking the first drink or hit; the body feels good (a good result!), but they suffer many consequences later.

Escaping the grasp of addiction requires a whole new way of thinking, but the point is that you can have either an addiction, or a good habit. You'll know you're in deep shit if you start racking up dark consequences and still have a compulsion to continue the behaviour. That is the point at which the behaviour's returns diminish greatly, and it begins to control your mind. If the update that created the addiction is not making you happy, you have to download a new one.

A final thought: there are no positive addictions, but what would happen if real happiness was an addiction?

Fear

Fear is an unpleasant feeling created by a sense of threat. All too often, however, that threat is imaginary, based on past experiences rather than the current reality. Because the fear is based in your imagination, the mind can choose to magnify or diminish it. The more creative the mind, the more the fear can be upgraded to a higher level and turn into a potential phobia. The stronger the past memory, the stronger the feeling it will create going forward.

Through my experience I have met so many academics and highly knowledgeable minds, and the level of fear they show towards new updates can be off the scale; they will overanalyse and over-evaluate every single scenario possible.

There are three types of fear that we experience when we update:

- Fear of losing something
- Fear when updating
- Fear of the upload.

Let's apply this to a scenario close to my heart. When I was considering leaving my teaching career at the highest level, I feared what I would be losing: a secure profession with a clear progression path ahead and opportunities to be promoted, time off during the holidays with my family, and the choice of not working at weekends and bank holidays. Most of the minds in my old school voiced all the possible losses: *you're going to miss the holidays, your pension will be affected, you will miss the steady income.* I now realise that their thinking was based on their dark imagination rather than the reality. By contrast, all the minds I met who were entrepreneurs were connected to reality, and they offered me a more rounded view: *you will have more freedom, but that comes at a cost of more accountability and responsibility.* They were living in the reality of an entrepreneur rather than the imagination, which allowed them to express the possible gains from the update as well as the losses.

The fear was reduced once I focused on what I could **gain** and **not** what I could **lose**. During a dark day at work with piles of marking and hundreds of emails, something in my head triggered a burst of energy: I realised that I felt trapped, and I had no freedom with my time. What could I gain from leaving? The simple answer was time freedom. I had an opportunity to escape the daily rat race and work when I wanted to; to have control of my time, my updates and my personal development. It was time to feel uncomfortable, and I embraced the fear rather than fearing it.

To control and manage your fear you have to be connected to reality, the present, the current, and disconnect with your imagination of the future and the memories of the past. The imagination is highly likely to create a dark mindset about the future, and focus on the possible losses based on past memories. We are wired not to lose whatever we still have and be comfortable with the present. But if you update your reality and allow your imagination to focus on the possible gains, the light mindset will realise that there are unlimited possibilities; the fear level will be reduced and the new update will replace the old memory.

Once I left teaching and started my own business, the next wave of fear entered my mind. The fear was about the process of updating from a *working* mindset to a *leading* mindset and having full control and accountability for my decisions. The process of updating is very, very painful for your emotions and self-belief, as you are failing more than you are winning. The only way I dealt with this and kept faith with the process was to reframe *failing* as *learning*. If learning was easy, everyone would be doing it and there would be nothing to learn. The more painful the learning, the more value the update will have and the greater the purpose it will bring to myself and the business.

The positive aspect of this type of fear is that it reduces the more you update; the faster you update, the faster the fear will reduce. You have control over the speed of the updating and the frequency of the updates.

The third type of fear is the fear of the upload: was it worth it? How would you feel if you found that the grass had indeed been greener on the other side? I did wonder what might have happened if I had stayed in the teaching profession. Would I have been a successful leader in the school, even become a head teacher? Perhaps I could have been an agent for positive change in education? But when these dark thoughts entered my mind, I programmed myself to remember why I left teaching in the first place: to achieve *time freedom*. That is the perspective I wanted, and that is the measure to my success.

When we fear what we have lost rather than what we can gain, we need to change the perspective:

- If I quit alcohol, I will have more money and I will have a clearer mind in the morning to…
- If I stop buying clothes every week, I will have money and time to…
- If I try playing a new sport, I will enjoy the process of meeting new people and…
- If I stop going out every Saturday night, I will be able to enjoy more quality time with…
- If I reduce screen time on my phone, I could…
- If I leave work on time, I could enjoy more time…

The fear is only a perspective, so shift your focus to the expected gains rather than the losses that could have been.

Concentrate on the present reality, not your imagination and past experiences.

● ● ● ● ●

We have looked at *passive* and *active* coping strategies; let's now return to the last two elements of PADD: *denial* and *delay*.

Another word for denial is *avoidance*; it is as if the person has decided that there is no stressor, and therefore there is no need for them to change behaviour, perception, or emotional response. The only way the individual can deal with this situation is to 'forget' it, or distract themself from trying to deal with it, by over-socialising, overconsuming and over-living. Denial can also result from a sense that, although the situation is indeed stressful, it can never be changed.

When travelling by plane, you are required to put your phone into flight mode during the trip; this is a setting that suspends radio-frequency signal transmission by the device, thereby disabling Bluetooth, telephony, and Wi-Fi. In this mode, the phone is like a person who copes by stopping communication with the outside world while still functioning normally in their own world, believing that they can cope with their emotions on their own.

You might also choose to switch your phone to silent mode. In emotional terms, this is comparable to shutting yourself down to the outside world, both internally and externally, not sharing your emotions and feelings and trying to deal with them on your own but not being able to function normally in the world.

This can be a trigger for an episode of depression involving low mood, feelings of hopelessness, low self-esteem, lack of energy and problems with sleep. In silent mode the phone alerts you to its presence by vibrating; this is like the continuous fluctuation of your emotions, creating ripples such as self-harm, which is usually a way of coping with or expressing overwhelming emotional distress.

The most common avoidance technique is substance abuse, which can be defined as a pattern of harmful use of any substance for mood-altering purposes. This coping strategy changes your mood to fun, relaxed or confident, or just reduces the anxiety of the problem. Overconsuming alcohol, social media, drugs and even food can become accepted behaviour when you are avoiding your situation; they represent a short-term fix, an attempt to chase that buzz that you feel you are missing out on. This solution avoids the problem by isolating the mind and making it dependent on something, dark or light.

Using substances to cope with difficult feelings may seem like an easier path for some, as these are accepted in the Western world: a drink after work, a blowout on a Friday night, a cheeky afternoon drink at the weekend. In the worst-case situation, this could lead to an addiction which is the opposite of connection. The dark mind will not be able to bear to be in the present in their own life, so it will isolate the thought processes and connect to something that will artificially alter the mind.

Like the passive coping strategies we looked at earlier, *delay* is a form of deflection. It is as if the person has decided that the situation is not important and therefore there is no need to deal with it immediately. Delay can also result from a sense that, although the situation is indeed stressful, it can wait to be resolved.

Denial and delay strategies may be appropriate stopgap measures, such as when the stress is so acute that to acknowledge it immediately would be overwhelming. This is when you shut down your emotions or disconnect from the situation. But you need to be aware that failing to make any decision now can create even more anxiety later. It's like your computer being affected by a virus; you might see a few pop-ups at first, but after a while every session is interrupted by a pop-up. The delay strategy has amplified the problem, so future solutions need to be amplified too; at first antivirus software would have been the fix, but now the hardware is affected and it may have to be taken into a computer shop for a reboot or, in the worst case, a replacement.

When you are dealing with your mental health, patience and time are not always the way to make it better; the solution has to be here and now. We're all evolving, and the world is evolving even quicker. This is just the start; each moment is a new beginning. There's no need to live for the future and believe things will just get better, because *future* is merely a concept in your head. When it arrives, it will be the present moment. If you're not living in the here and now, you'll miss it. You'll keep dreaming about a new you, which never really comes as you are not investing in any new updates and just replicating the old ones that were tried and tested. The past experiences and dark updates just do not add any value to your future unless you update because of them.

During my encounters with people whose minds had become disconnected, with some of them ending up homeless, I realised that there were two kinds of mindsets that would cope with the dark mind in different ways. There were those that would stay dark; these were the individuals that connected with drugs like spice and alcohol so they did not need to deal with the demons that existed in their minds. They keep connecting with the dark updates and disconnect with any new updates. In contrast, many of the volunteers who were supporting the homeless organisations had been mostly dark-minded to begin with and had experienced some sort of tremor, but changed to a lighter mind to support and serve others in greater need.

We all have challenges in our life, but that's okay. Say yes to life. Accept what's here and now. Trust life, even if it doesn't look the way you want it to. The problem isn't life, but your expectations and perception of it.

Keep searching

How can you create your own light and your own direction in life?

The morning after my dad died eight years ago (2012), I was walking down the path in front of my home, the same one I had walked down the night before, and it suddenly dawned on me how different my thoughts were in the daylight. My perception of the situation changed, even though the situation remained the same.

Last night, I'd been walking down the path late at night and I'd been slightly scared, walking fast, and confused about the situation; but venturing down the same path this morning, I was walking leisurely, strolling along and not once considering looking for someone behind me. It dawned on me that that's the difference between night and day, between darkness and light. This is something that's probably happened to all of us at some point. We've walked somewhere at night and felt entirely differently when we walked down the very same path during the day. It's amazing what a little light, a little change of perspective, a little more ability to see where we're going, can do.

To me, this is a great example of how our minds (coupled with external conditions) can transform the world. The path I was walking down was the exact same path. Same path. Same grass. Same distance from the road to the door. Nothing had changed overnight. Yet, now, in the morning light, I was seeing it differently, imagining how my mum and my sister would be feeling and how I would need to be the bright light for my family from now on.

And seeing this path differently made me think about the way I see my life differently too. When I realised what a difference the daylight made in my perception of the path, I really got to thinking about my own internal 'day' and 'night', the light and dark within my own mind. As I stepped off the path and into my car, to go and visit my grieving mum, my mind was flooded with questions. That was the ignition for me not to grieve.

What if we applied this idea of light and dark to the paths of our lives? What if we realised, really understood, that we could be walking down the same path and see it entirely differently? What if this is the path for me and it will make me stronger? How will I shine light on others more than myself?

What if we realised that we have the ability to transform the blackness into light? To transform a situation with the light we shed on it?

Of course, these are not just ideas. People have more or less always known that the way we think about things, and how much metaphorical darkness or light we give to a situation, impacts the world around us. Our mindsets are powerful, powerful things and we can truly alter our worlds with our thoughts and actions. We can change things in both negative and positive ways; and more importantly, we can **control** how we change them. We have the ability to cast more light or more darkness on a situation, depending on the solution we desire.

For example, when walking alone at night, I can frighten myself terribly if I start thinking of all the dangerous things that could happen or revisiting terrifying situations I've heard about. Conversely, when walking along on a beautiful day, the sun shining brightly overhead, I can convince myself that I don't have a care in the world. Even though I might be having a bad day, for just a few moments the warm sunshine pouring down on me can transform my mood because it causes me to think of summer, warmth, happiness. My mind takes what it sees out in the world and transforms it, labelling it, using it to create a dark or light mindset.

When I realised how much my mind could transform the world around me, I began thinking about how I could increase the light in my life. For instance, when walking at night, I could have brought a flashlight, to light up the path before me. If I had the power to, I could install lighting alongside the path, creating a well-lit walk. And these ideas tie in perfectly with what I'm always writing about: the *effort* it takes to be a positive person. It takes work, energy, and effort to have a path that is shining bright. But, as anyone who has walked down a well-lit path wrapped in a feeling of safety knows, it's worth the effort if you are able to navigate the path unafraid.

If you're anything like me, that's the feeling you want. You want to be unafraid. You want to walk down roads and paths that are well-lit. You want to see clearly and not be scared and feel safe. So how do you do that?

Let's start the update differently.

● ● ● ● ●

How do you make the path of your life a path that is lit up, limitless and drowning out fear while at the same time finding a balance between the darkness and the light?

As we all know, you cannot live in bright, blinding light forever. Light is wonderful. It helps us to see and helps us to thrive and grow. But without darkness, we would have no patience and would just be running quickly into the light with no real purpose. We need the darkness as well as the light. We need a path that is lit the way many streets are: with the light and dark intertwined, allowing us to see without brightening the world to an unnatural state.

We need both the light and the dark in our lives, but there are ways we can make our paths brighter, ways we can make the road we're travelling down just a little bit clearer. Here are five ways to shed more light on that path of yours...

1. **Bring your own source of light**

If you know you're going to be walking down a dark path, bring your own light. So what does that mean? It means you create your own light where there is darkness; that is how you shed light on it. Look at it from new angles, shine light into the dark corners and look deep within yourself for a positive light. You don't have to wait around for someone to turn a light on for you, or to rescue you from the darkness; in fact, more often than not, light isn't just going to beam down on you for no reason.

If you're on a dark path, you have to create light or, better yet, you have to *be* the light. Don't wait for it; *be* it.

2. Surround yourself with others

Ever notice how a dark path isn't nearly as frightening when you're with other people? Walking down a dark road alone can be difficult, but it's a lot less terrifying when you surround yourself with others. Life's kind of like that too. It can be scary and overwhelming at times, but when you surround yourself with people (especially positive and light-minded people), the dark road before you seems a little brighter, a little easier to bear. It can still be tough, but I know that I feel a lot safer on a dark road with a group of friends than I do when I'm on my own. Surrounding yourself with a great support system will help make even the most dimly lit path seem safe enough to walk down.

So start the conversation. Find the light around you. If you can't see it, you're looking in the wrong direction. The world is made up of some amazing people that light up their own lives and are happy to light up yours; you just have to find them and see how their light will surround you. Too many people are looking for the light to come to them – it doesn't work like that!

3. Choose your route carefully

It would be nice if we could always walk in sunshine, but we know that's not the case. We will all have to walk in the dark sometimes, stumbling and unsure of where we're headed. But don't look down and give up. Instead, look around you and see if this really is the best path to be on.

Sometimes all it takes is opening your eyes and looking around to see that nearby is another, brighter path which many people have walked on before you. But you have to question whether that is the right or bright path for you, or whether you are just following other people's light as it seems easier at the time. This is where some minds lose their purpose and passion and become dark as they are following other people's light from social media stories and fake celebrity lifestyles. They are focusing on the light rather than the route, on the outcome rather than the process.

Everyone's path is different, and the time that people have walked in the dark or the light differs too, so occasionally we're forced in one direction; but often we have a choice. We can choose the path we want to go down. We can look for the brightest path and, if we don't see a bright path, we can make our own paths; but the key is not to stay too long on the dark path of uncertainty and fear, and to find a path that makes you happy.

4. Imagine a light solution

You're probably familiar with the Law of Attraction and, though I won't go into the details here, I find the concept appealing. I really do believe that we can attract things with our thoughts. Therefore, if you think the path you're on is going to get darker and darker, it will.

So, imagine the best! Imagine the sky lightening and the sun peeking out from behind the clouds. Imagine bumping into a friendly group of people along your path. Don't think of all the negative things that could happen or you will attract them to you; stop the buffering. Instead, think of the wonderful things you'll encounter on your journey, and you **will** encounter them. You must go and create these opportunities and connect with people and experiences that will show you a brighter path.

5. Be prepared for the dark

Even with all your positive thinking and imagining the best, sometimes things don't go as well as planned. Sometimes the batteries in your flashlight die. Sometimes all your friends have to head down a different path and you're on your own again. Don't despair! Instead, be prepared. If possible, it's ideal to have some self-defence skills under your belt. If you can prepare yourself by strengthening your skills, you'll be more likely to travel safely down your path. I really believe that the more self-confidence you have and the less self-doubt, the less likely you are to get attacked. Same thing goes for life. Be confident, believe in yourself, and you're a lot less likely to be brought down by others' dark minds.

Life is filled with light and dark: perfectly lit paths and dark, winding roads. We're all aware of the good and the bad, but we don't always remember that we can make the most of the darkness and, in fact, we can make even the darkest times brighter if we choose to take any of the actions I've mentioned above. You, me, we all can shed light on our own paths, to make the roads we're travelling down brighter. And, awesomely enough, we also can shed light on the paths of others as well. Give some thought to how you can brighten your own path – and how you can give others a little bit of that bright light too.

Update Six
Disruption of happiness

THE WORD 'HAPPINESS' is used to mean a pleasant mental or emotional state, ranging from contentment to intense joy. It is also used in the context of life satisfaction, flourishing and well-being (which may be subjective). The happiness we pursue may never be reached, but we are more likely to enjoy happiness by creating the conditions that it can flourish in.

Your mental health affects your overall health more than you may realise. When you are stressed out, angry, or sad, your body suffers too: whether it be in the form of digestive issues, headaches, back pain, or any number of other physical symptoms. Most people I meet every day want to improve their well-being and increase their daily happiness; but we need to value patience regarding the journey, as we are all looking for 'fast happiness'.

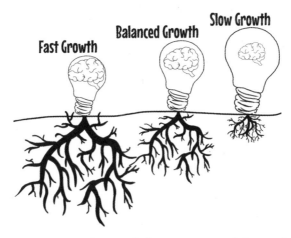

We need to understand the processes of *fast* and *slow* happiness, and we'll come to that in a moment. Before we move on, however, let's consider fast and slow thinking. Fast thinking can be spontaneous, and decisions are made with emotion; slow thinking is more purposeful and more rational. Fast thinking allows us to grow, but it also reveals the pervasive influence of the outside world and how it can affect or distort our thoughts and behaviours, which makes it difficult to predict what will make us happy in the future as the circumstances may have changed. When can we trust our intuition, and when can we not? We need to understand how we can tap into the benefits of slow thinking, which offers practical and enlightening insights into how choices are made in our personal lives – and how we can use different techniques to guard against the mental glitches that make us dark-minded.

So, what are the actions and behaviours that will contribute to our mental happiness, and what is going to hinder it? Adrian will adopt the behaviours of SLOW happiness, and Dawn will try to behave using the FAST strategy of happiness. Let's consider Adrian's approach first.

S – Selfish

Adrian will only think about his own happiness; the world revolves around him. Selfish people don't know they're being selfish – they just assume they're nice people who care about their own happiness more than anything else. But on their journey towards finding their happiness, they carelessly and intentionally walk over people.

Unfortunately, the traits of selfish people are not easy to notice. Most of the time, they are people pleasers and hide their dark mind very well. Selfish people are skilled manipulators by instinct and control freaks at heart. Manipulative people truly believe that their way of handling a situation is the only way because it means that their needs are being met, and that's all that matters. They always experience FOMO as they are always chasing someone else's dreams and lives.

L – Labels and loneliness

Why are people so obsessed with certain labels? Most people have a desire to fit in, whether at school, work or in social circles. For this reason, they sometimes buy particular products because they believe the labels will contribute to greater social acceptance. Consumers often buy clothing brands that are perceived as fashionable, trendy or high class, or that fit into a particular subculture or peer group. The 'keeping up with the Patels' mentality epitomises this brand-buying motive.

In 2010 the World Health Organisation surveyed 89,000 people from eighteen countries, and found that depression was more likely to hit those living in high-income communities than poorer communities. The research indicates that a desire for wealth and possessions is linked to a need to mask inner discontent. Some people value floor space over friend space. The continual striving for greater wealth and material possessions leads to unhappiness, because we can neither satisfy the desires nor change the reasons behind them.

Adrian is attached to the labels as they increase his self-worth at the detriment of his self-confidence and self-esteem. He is not flexible in his thinking and gets his way in whatever way he can; he tries to be self-reliant, but he is attached to people around him.

Adrian assumes most new people he meets can't be trusted. Unfortunately this behaviour slowly starts to close the door on any connection outside of an inner circle and any chances of meeting new friends, and this in turn creates social isolation and loneliness. Adrian's dark-mindedness only attracts other dark-minded people in his circle; his thinking limits his own growth.

O – Outcomes and others

Adrian tends to micromanage in his desire to control all outcomes, and falls apart in dramatic fashion when life throws a wrench in his plan. He always experiences FOMO, and fears the real FOMO which is the fear of moving on.

Adrian believes that someone else's good fortune steals from his own outcomes. He lives under the illusion that there's only a finite amount of success to go around, and constantly compares his own growth against theirs. This leads to jealousy and resentment. His success is only measured by his own KPIs (key performance indicators). His outcomes are limited as they only have external value gained through approval from others, rather than the internal value of happiness and contentment.

W – What's wrong with the world

There's plenty wrong with this world, no arguments here. Yet Adrian focuses *only* on what's wrong and turns a blind eye to what's actually right in the world. You can spot him a mile away: he'll be the one complaining and responding to any positive attributes of our world with 'yeah but'. He always sees the world as being full of dangers and pitfalls; yes, that is true, but Adrian amplifies them without any real justification. He believes that all of society and the world is against him and that his own decisions and actions are always the right ones. The dark mind creates a constant buffering and is always identifying problems rather than searching for solutions.

Let's consider a situation where Adrian is visiting a new city for the first time with a group of friends. He will try and take control of the weekend by booking and reserving the best restaurants and bars in the city to his own thinking and liking, not for a second considering the others. He will only visit the shops that he usually buys from and will not be willing to try anything new with his friends. His outcomes are already pre-installed and ready to be edited and manipulated for social media. He creates uncertainty and doubt all weekend as he is searching for any problems that he could bring to the surface and exploit.

● ● ● ● ●

Now let's look at Dawn's strategy and consider how you could adopt FAST happiness in your life.

F – Fuel

Living a healthy lifestyle and fuelling your body with the right ingredients is key to achieving your optimal mental happiness and well-being. A healthy lifestyle is simply ensuring that you eat and drink well and effectively manage your stress. It's a lifestyle, not a diet.

Maintaining these simple rules every day will transform your physical appearance magnificently. Other than improving the quality of your life, it also makes you healthy and happy emotionally. However, living a healthy lifestyle can mean something different depending on an individual. A healthy life or healthy living habits should be a daily routine, not a temporary event that occurs when you have enough time to spare. Consider what foods suit your body and what are the dietary requirements that make *you* feel and be happier.

Currently the world is full of convenience food options but drinking water and eating fresh fruit and vegetables is always a good start on a happier and healthier journey. Dawn uses many of the solutions available regarding how you fuel yourself on a daily basis, but the key points are control and discipline. We are all attracted by indulgences and fast food, but happy food is slow food. Discipline yourself so that the fuel that enters your body is only slow, happy food. Your food choices each day affect your health: how you feel today, tomorrow, and in the future. Good fuel, or good nutrition, is an important part of leading a healthy lifestyle.

The link between good nutrition and healthy weight, reduced risk of chronic disease, and overall health is too important to ignore. By taking steps to eat healthily, you'll be on your way to getting the nutrients your body needs to stay healthy, active, and strong. Health is wealth.

A – Active

Being active is picking the longer and harder journey; for example, walking rather than taking the car, or even taking the stairs rather than the lift. Happiness is being active rather than being inactive. There is no quick fix, as the active journey is more painful and difficult; the key update is to keep moving forward and make choices that keep you moving and being active.

Exercise has been linked to improved mental health and cognitive function, with a number of studies having found that exercise helps mental happiness. There are many views as to how exercise helps people with their mental health. Being active can block negative thoughts or distract you from daily worries. Increased fitness will lift your mood and improve sleep patterns, whilst exercise can also change levels of chemicals in your brain, such as serotonin, endorphins and stress hormones.

It also creates opportunities for increased social contact, especially playing team sports. This supports the notion that happiness is greatest within a tribal setting; we are more content when we share in an activity with others. A good example of this is the parkrun movement. People have always run in parks, but the weekly parkrun gets people running together and in this it has a sense of purpose: to have fun, gain experience or just talk to each other.

S – Social connection

Social connection is the experience of feeling close and connected to others; it involves feeling loved, cared for and valued. I believe it to be a core human need, and it is a fundamental driver for growth and happiness. We are tribal animals, and having a well-connected society depends on light-minded people that create meaningful and quality relationships.

Connection is the energy that is needed to drive collaboration and communication and make people come together for a purpose. In our modern society we celebrate everything from every wedding anniversary to baby graduations, but we are missing the fundamental element that they all have in common which is meaningful *purpose* for everyone. A true light connection should create more value, more energy and more connection to everyone that attends; that's why social revolutions like parkrun and Big Sleep Out have had huge uptake in the world as they give more. Maximise the connections with purpose to maximise the light energy that it creates for yourself and others.

Look up, Light up, Meet up...

T – Thinking

Thinking is the ultimate cognitive activity: consciously using our brains to make sense of the world around us and decide how to respond to it. While many people believe that our feelings precede (or are independent of) our thoughts, the truth is that our feelings are products of our thoughts. This revelation can be both daunting and liberating; daunting because it makes us responsible for our attitudes, and liberating because we have the power to choose our perspective, mood and thoughts.

When we are aware that we can choose and direct our thinking, we realise that we have the ability to better control the circumstances of our lives, improve our decision-making processes and generally live brighter lives.

Steps to think faster and lighter:
1. Identify the problem. The first task is to determine if a problem exists. Sometimes, when you think it through, you may come to the conclusion that there isn't a problem at all, just a misunderstanding. If

that's the case, fine. If not, and you determine that there is indeed a problem, you need to identify exactly what it is. When someone weighs the pros and cons of a problem systematically, and is able to see how clearly they can define and state it, that is an indication of a highly developed intelligence.

2. Analyse the problem. Once you've determined the problem, look at it from a variety of perspectives. Is it solvable? Is it real or perceived? Can you solve it alone or do you need help? Sometimes, by looking at it from many angles you can come up with a light resolution right away. You may also reveal a biased view that needs to be broadened or enlightened by a new update.

3. Brainstorm and come up with several possible solutions. Problems can be solved in many ways. Write down anything that comes to mind and then go over the list and narrow it down to the best possibilities. Having several viable options leads to obtaining the best results.

4. Decide which solution fits well. Go over your list of possible solutions. Different situations call for different solutions. Quite often what works in one situation may not work in a similar one. Take time to determine what will work best for the problem at hand. One solution usually does not fit all.

5. Take action. Implement your solution. Every problem has a solution, even if it is to accept the situation and move on. Instead of approaching problems and challenges as insurmountable obstacles, we can

view them as opportunities to hone our critical thinking and problem-solving skills. It may not be the right solution at the time, but keep updating and keep finding that solution for a happier outcome.

Every problem we are able to resolve increases self-confidence and self-worth. Thinking critically not only helps us handle future challenges more skilfully, it also broadens our life experience and helps us gain perspective. Faster thinking does not mean making quick decisions; it's more about making ***better*** decisions.

Update Seven
Lighten the mind through the CRACK

TOO MANY PEOPLE are busy making a living, not designing their life; but before you can start focusing on the design you must first create your map of where you are today. Only then can you make the life you desire and deserve, by closing the gap from where you are to where you want to be.

The *wheel of light* is a way to visualise each element of your life and rate its relative quality level, so you can uncover which areas need updating more than others. The wheel is divided into ten rays, which  are the areas where scientific research suggests we can take practical actions to boost well-being. Within each ray of light, different things work for different people at different times, so we need a selection by priority rather than a full range of actions.

Each section has three steps:

 Look up – Reflect on your current situation.

 Light up – Plan what you would like to do and find a solution.

 Fix up – Take action and start the first steps to a lighter future.

CRACK and STARS

Light needs cracks to shine through on our journey of life…

 … and we need stars to guide us on the dark days of the process.

I have divided the ten rays making up the wheel of light into two groups of five which I'll call CRACK and STARS. Thus we have two key areas to develop and on which to focus our light and energy. The CRACK may be your primary focus and the STARS can be your secondary focus, but it does not matter as you really need to consider both sides of the wheel. That's the biggest challenge: to focus on *all* the rays of light and try to balance your happiness.

We'll look at the STARS in the next chapter, but first of all let's turn our attention to the CRACK.

| Connect | Reckless | Active | Care | Keep learning |

C – Connect with empathy and compassion

Life's biggest moments and experiences are found in your connections with others. It's easy to think you have it all, when you are shining with a single beam of light. Relationships require time and energy; you're called upon to practise the art of empathy and compassion. Yet it's through your connections to other people that you find happiness. Deepen your relationships with friends, family, your partner, peers, and your community using these tips.

Look up: make time to connect

In today's world, there's a bigger emphasis on running around and getting things done than there is on making time to connect with others. Look at your weekly calendar and schedule a date night with your partner, a lunch or activity with a friend, and some quiet time for yourself to simply be still and reflect. You may be surprised at how making time to connect with others shifts the quality of your relationships. You may also feel the shift in how you relate with others as a result of carving out time to be with yourself.

Light up: change the mindset to listen

Pay attention to how you listen to others. Perhaps you hear them speak but you don't really listen to what they say. While you listen, are you already formulating your response? Do you have a tendency to finish their sentences or to interrupt them with your own experiences? Are you listening to your own internal dialogue and making assumptions or judgments about the other person? When you can listen from your heart rather than your head, you're able to be present while someone else shares. When you feel heard – really heard – by another, it deepens your level of trust and connection with them.

Another profound way to connect with others is to dip below the surface and explore the deeper conversations that reveal other people's likes and dislikes. Everyone has things that work for them and things that don't. Everyone has things that they need in certain relationships, and boundaries that, when crossed, have the potential to compromise friendships, destroy family ties, and disintegrate working relationships. Ask people what's important to them and what things would cause them to reconsider being in a relationship with you, and vice versa.

The 4F model encourages you to promote new links within your circle. This is great for personal growth, from finding people to play a sport with to looking for a new job opportunity. Consider these four different types of connection:

- Friends ➜ Friends
- Friends ➜ Family
- Family ➜ Friends
- Family ➜ Family

Think how you could grow your own circle, and how you are connected within your circle, using the model above. Update your circle of contacts and see how you update your mind.

Fix up: actively show empathy and compassion

People that demonstrate *empathy* are the best people to connect with. When was the last time someone asked you about *you*? The art of actively showing empathy happens when you turn empathy into a verb instead of simply viewing it as a state. Practise the ability to understand and share the feelings of another person. Ask people about their lives, their families, their hobbies, goals and visions. Then, really listen to what they have to say. Spend time relating with them through body language, facial expressions, and your overall quality of presence. Be there with them in that moment. Refrain from checking your phone and other mindless distractions.

How you interact directly with others affects the energy of the relationship. When you give your full attention to the person you're with, it enhances your connection. Dawn will actively connect with people on a regular basis by visiting them face to face and dropping a WhatsApp message to ask how things are going; but what makes him really different from Adrian is that he has *compassion*. He shows kindness, care, and a willingness to help others when everyone is just helping themselves.

Relationships require open, compassionate and conscious communication. Effective communication asks that you show up in the conversation without engaging in melodrama or blaming others or yourself. Instead employ heartfelt, open dialogue between people. When you can share how you feel about something, while requesting help from that person to meet your needs, it provides both sides with an opportunity to practise mindful communication.

Through your own personal update, you come to know and understand yourself at a deeper level. As this journey unfolds, you inevitably learn more about those who play a role in your life experiences. You can explore where your beliefs and behaviours were first imprinted if you place attention on your emotions as they rise up to the surface in challenging situations. When you can recognise that your old patterns and beliefs no longer support you, you have an opportunity to perceive, and live, life differently. This type of realisation allows you to see that others are also doing their best from their level of awareness in this moment and from their perspective. Knowing this makes it easier to let go of grievances.

Be around people different from you. It's easy to get tunnel vision when you surround yourself **only** with people from the same background, geography, or life stage. Leave your comfort zone and make friends with people you least expect. You'll be surprised at how much you might learn and update.

R – Real adventure

'Life is inherently risky. There is only one big risk you should avoid at all costs, and that is the risk of doing nothing.' – Denis Waitley

So what is real adventure? Humans have a strange, almost biologically coded need to *believe*. We have particular beliefs about the workings of the world, religion, people and yes, *travel* too – for example, the belief that certain places in the world are dangerous and other places are safer.

According to a work published in 2002 by a noted expert on shark attacks, worldwide each year around 150 people are killed by falling coconuts, in contrast to the number of shark-caused deaths per year which is around five. So when it comes to life experiences, do we all fear real adventure because of the imagined risk and just default to the comfortable and safe choice?

Adventurous experiences create psychological *arousal* which can be interpreted negatively as *fear* or positively as *excitement*. I remember dreaming for years about travelling the world. First it was a ferry trip to France as it was the nearest coast and the only foreign adventure my parents could afford. Then it was the United States with a thirty-day unlimited flight pass, because it seemed like the land of dreams for me and my family. We arrived at the airport and picked the first flight out, and just rang up hotels from the arrivals lounge. We had no plan, no strategy, no accommodation, no car; but crossing America from east to west and experiencing the best that the country could offer – this was my first experience of *real* adventure.

Some people are programmed to enjoy the fake world of adventure, with all-inclusives and planned tour guides. Why not opt instead for the flexibility and fun of real, limitless adventure?

Look up: explore yourself

You can become an everyday explorer without leaving your home and loved ones behind. I believed adventures only awaited in exotic places. Then my eyes were opened to the truth: everywhere is somewhere. Take a different route to work; you've no idea what you'll discover. Take a sabbatical from your usual haunts at the weekend and try somewhere unknown. Forget TripAdvisor – just get out there and roam freely. Don't plan anything. I never book restaurants; I adopt the simple strategy and just look for the busiest restaurant, or where the locals eat.

Light up: explore the world

You've no idea what you're capable of until you try. Say *yes* to things you might have previously said *no* to. Try your hand at a different sport, or join something you would never have imagined doing.

One evening eight years ago, my family and I were sitting around the table discussing how we would celebrate my brother-in-law's fortieth birthday. The regular adventures were suggested: Vegas, Miami, even Ibiza – yes, it was going to be a crazy lads' holiday – but the conversation and tone changed when he mentioned the word *Kilimanjaro*. Most people around the table didn't even know about it, so everyone started Googling.

As the drinks flowed and the night went on, it became the number one conversation topic for a group of old British Asian men who had never climbed a mountain before, let alone the highest mountain in Africa. *Let's start with climbing Snowdon and see how everyone feels*? We had unlocked the mind, and the journey started.

So a new WhatsApp group was born with whole new discussions on boots, gaiters, Gore-Tex and even talcum powder… we were entering a whole new world. We were more excited about trips to GO Outdoors than going to watch the football at the pub; it's strange to think how our mindsets changed for a new purpose. We took different groups to Snowdonia, Scafell Pike and Yorkshire's Three Peaks. The experience and the conversations were amazing, our mental happiness was in good condition and we were all physically fitter; we all were focusing on the task ahead with a clearer and lighter mind.

Finally, in August 2012, D-Day arrived: the Kili 13 team was born, and we were all booked to go for this great adventure. The experience was one of the best we ever had. It was the darkest place we have ever been, both mentally and physically; but we all rose from the ashes and became stronger from the experience. The achievement was not getting to the top but enjoying the trek together. It was a double celebration for me as my second daughter was born three days into the trek. ☺ The biggest challenge is to say *yes* and work it out later.

Fix up: explore your mind

So how do we start this process of real adventure and free the mind? You need to find the answers within you, not by following what others do on social media. And that's the challenge: you need an adventure with a real purpose that comes from *your own* aspirations and heightened expectations. Your insecurities are the jail to your freedom. What did you want to do and where did you want to go when you were younger? Or maybe just connect with a destination or activity because it means something to you?

A great example is that, when I talk to honeymoon couples, they all mention the same destinations: Bora Bora, Bali, the Maldives, Mauritius… it's a default setting. They want the picture-perfect postcard to send home to the family to signal that their relationship is perfect, like their holiday. Breaking it down, most couples spend three times more on their honeymoon than on their average holiday; but the question is, do they gain three times the value? Also, if it was such an amazing experience, why do they not make repeat trips to these destinations more often?

What do I mean by a real adventure? It's a real feeling, an unusual and exciting or daring experience that will challenge your mind; a trip to somewhere you connect with and will gain value from when you come back. You don't spend half the holiday getting that perfect picture; you just enjoy the experience and capture every moment for yourself. Dawn is always going on different types of experiences – city breaks, beach holidays, activity breaks, challenges, attending new courses – while Adrian goes on lots of similar holidays, having similar experiences with similar outcomes; the all-inclusive package with planned tours is all he wants.

When planning an adventure, the *why* is so important; so please ask yourself these five questions and make sure your next ***real*** adventure has purpose and value:

- Why do you want to see it or do it?
- What will you gain from the experience?
- Will you grow from this experience?
- Does the experience challenge you?
- Do you own your experience?

Good luck with your next ***real*** adventure – it could change your mindset forever. Once you have experienced the feeling of growth, you will want more of it. Don't make it an occasional fix, but part of your lifestyle and the choices you make every day. Update with real adventure.

A – Active with fuel

Being active and fuelling your body with the right ingredients is key to achieving your optimal mental and physical well-being. A healthy lifestyle is not difficult; it is not something that you want to spend your whole life dreaming about. It's simply ensuring that you do regular exercise, eat well and effectively manage your stress. It's a lifestyle, not a diet.

Maintaining these simple rules every day will transform your physical appearance magnificently, and also make you healthy emotionally. However, living a healthy lifestyle can mean something different depending on an individual. It should be a daily routine, not a temporary event that occurs when you have time to spare. Once you start practising healthy habits, you will automatically feel and experience the good results of maintaining them.

Look up: are you active, and what's your fuel?

Let's consider how you fuel yourself; that means *what* do you eat and *where* do you eat, in or out? There is a simple model that has been effective in light-minded people to discipline your fuel intake: it's the 7-7-7 rule.

You have 21 meal occasions in a week, based on the 7-7-7 rule – that is, three meals a day over a seven-day week. So, reflecting on your food and drink habits, what would they look like:

	Breakfast	In/out	Lunch	In/out	Dinner	In/out
Monday						
Tuesday						
Wednesday						
Thursday						
Friday						
Saturday						
Sunday						

Completing this table will help you to see how you fuel yourself on a weekly basis: the balance between the dark fuel of eating out and the light fuel of eating in and controlling the intake to your personal needs.

Now let's consider how active you are. The same rule applies: the 7-7-7 rule. Reflect on your activity during the week, in each part of the day. Try to measure how taxing each activity is, for example do you walk or run? Do a full gym workout or just steps?

	Morning	Afternoon	Evening
Monday			
Tuesday			
Wednesday			
Thursday			
Friday			
Saturday			
Sunday			

Light up : Be active and fuel well

We have seen that each week you have 21 occasions for meals and 21 opportunities to be active. The magic number here is 14, which is two-thirds of 21 or approximately 66%. If 66% of the habits and actions you are making every week are light-minded for a healthy lifestyle, this shows that the balance of your life is in your favour.

You have 86,400 seconds or 1,440 minutes per day to prepare what you eat and consider how you are going to be active. Preparing food at home is very important as you can control what you consume and customise portions to your needs. Try to be active 66% of the time, from walking to work, taking the stairs instead of the lift or just choosing an activity rather than being inactive.

Planning how you are going to live, in terms of how you fuel yourself and how active you are, is not a quick fix; it's a series of decisions about your lifestyle that you have to make for yourself. This book does not claim any expertise on health and well-being; you know your own body and what it needs to function to its fullest capacity.

Fix up your lifestyle

Changing your eating habits and your activity can be a challenge, but the easiest way is not to see it as something you have to do, but more a set of daily habits that you abide by. You're probably thinking, this is not going to be easy... so let's look at some of the real situations you're likely to encounter, and consider the decisions you may have to make in terms of Dawn and Adrian's mindsets.

Situation	Adrian	Dawn
Work colleagues going out for lunch	Eat with them	Still go out, eat early at work
Friends going out for drinks	Go rounds	Still go out, buy your own
Friday night dinner	Order takeaway	Eat in, make a quick meal
Dinner with colleagues	Over-consume	Share meals and enjoy
Free food/drink events	Over-consume	Eat what you enjoy
Shopping	No shopping list	List of items you like to eat
Schedule	No plan for the week	Plan for the day
Meals	Ready meals	Ready to cook in

Frozen	Frozen meals	Frozen ingredients
Stress	Overeat	Go for a walk or run
Fast food	Convenience	Functional treat
Home cooking	Limited options	Wide range of options
Walking	Chore	Habit
Exercise	Occasional	Lifestyle

Update your mind and update your mental and physical health.

C – Care for others (Share and Give)

'No one ever got poor by giving' – Anne Frank

Caring for others is an important part of maintaining relationships with people close to you. It can even bring you closer together. Helping, providing, feeding, reaching out, listening, protecting, looking after and hugging; all of the actions associated with caring require bravery and generosity, because they involve a lot of effort. Those who are less inclined to be caring toward others have a hard time understanding why caring people do these things. However, even though they can be difficult, they also bring us a lot of hidden benefits.

Being *caring* means providing a listening ear, noticing when someone needs help, and helping your community without asking for a reward. So look up and see where support and help is needed around you; your light will shine brighter when others shine too. Caring for others is really caring for ourselves.

Look up at how you give and share

It's time to look up and see who you can really care about. When you care for someone, the action itself isn't as important as the attitude that you have towards them.

The type of care needed is different depending on who or what is being cared for. You dress children, you may go to the gym, and water plants; you can even care for objects (like a car or a house), as well as abstract concepts (like ideologies and values), and it's always the same: you offer your time and dedication to protect them and make sure they don't become damaged or corrupted.

In this modern world we live in, do we care about our possessions and what people think of us more than the things of real value – the love and happiness we share with the people we are connected to? Do we care more about the number of likes we have on Facebook than the likes we receive when we care about others? The important thing is not to confuse *self-love* with *selfishness*. Selfish people only help others because it inflates their own ego; people who have self-love realise that if they first respect themselves, it will be much easier to respect others.

Here's a real-world example that shows how necessary it is to take care of ourselves so that we can take care of others. Aeroplane protocol dictates that when turbulence occurs and the oxygen masks fall, we should put our own on first, and then help our children with theirs. Is this the behaviour of a bad parent? Not at all. It means that you're taking care of your physical safety so that you can take care of the child, because if you didn't do it for yourself, nobody else would do it for you.

You can't try to spend hours upon sleepless hours taking care of a sick family member if you don't get any sleep. You need to be awake and able to pay attention to their needs. Don't feel guilty. You're not being selfish; it's the opposite. You're preparing yourself to help them in an intelligent, instead of desperate, manner.

Light up to the one we care about

We are all looking for our own happiness, but we can't find it or see it or create it for ourselves. So what is *real* giving? It's the habit of transferring something of benefit to someone else without expecting to receive something in return.

We are not programmed that way, as we give to receive: that's how the exchange process works in the world we live in. An exchange is simply when someone decides to satisfy a need or want in exchange for some money, or goods or services. We are programmed to enter into exchange relationships all the time in our everyday life. Real giving is more than simply tipping someone at a restaurant; it means giving your time and energy in a positive light.

Let's see Dawn's mindset. Here are some light-minded habits that we could adopt when we want to give:

- Just smiling to everyone you meet
- Looking back when you close a door
- Saying thank you
- Taking your glass back to the bar/counter when on a night out
- Giving up your seat on the bus for someone else
- Giving unwanted items to others that need them
- Not parking on double yellow lines or on pavements
- Sharing a meal with a friend/group
- Sharing and using your study notes together – it's called collaboration
- Car sharing when going to work
- Sharing a pizza at work
- Sharing on social media what really matters to you, such as your feelings and emotions.

How is Adrian thinking?

- Giving presents at Christmas and birthdays – creating an exchange process
- Giving presents on occasions like Valentine's Day – meeting an obligation
- Creating events not everyone can afford – being exclusive not inclusive
- Sharing on social media your location and what you are eating and drinking – influencing
- Reading your WhatsApp message (two blue ticks) and not responding – buffering.

Fix up: care for others

Can you develop a caring nature? Ask yourself a different question: what makes someone dark-hearted or selfish? It could be the environment in which they grew up, with 'hard' parents who never showed love or affection. It could be having difficult circumstances throughout life and developing a shell to avoid any further hurt or dark-mindedness. It could be due to feeling unloved and unwanted and needing to shield oneself from anything that could be hurtful. There could be a range of reasons why the mind has become a caring one or an uncaring one. But the update is to become caring around yourself and others around you.

Being very caring can be a difficult burden to bear. In many cases, the darker mind is very self-involved and self-interested. People are masterful at deflecting; in your vain attempts to care for them, you will often find that they turn it on you and make you the difficult one.

You have probably heard or read the research on the different roles people can play in social connection: a giver, taker, or matcher. Givers, well, they give a lot. Takers take a lot, and matchers try and keep score of the give and take. When it comes to caring, the people most likely to be there for you when you need them are, of course, the givers. They are the ones in life who can never do enough for those in need. Unfortunately, in many cases, they are attracted to takers. If this is you, you need to unlock the mindset, rate your level of contribution and giving every day, and create a light habit.

A concept I use is 'Oh, CRAP', which stands for Care, Reflect, Action, and Plan. This is the feeling that you get when you really think about someone else and you forget that you care for them; these steps will support your care for others. How does it work? Oh,

Care: who in my circle of friends and family have I neglected, or who needs the greatest care from me? Where can I maximise my impact and create time for this care?

Reflect on how you could contribute and give with compassion and empathy.

Action: start the conversation with this person or community.

Plan on how you are going to care for this person or community.

Your giving nature will be admirable and will probably help more people than you can count, but you need to take care of yourself and stop trying to change someone who doesn't want to change. Leopards are born leopards and won't change their spots. You can ignore their behaviour, stop being hurt by their actions, and turn your attention to something that really matters.

Embrace your new light mind. A light-minded giver can often be left feeling as though they are the weak one, or the stupid one. In fact, the dark-hearted giver will seem to enjoy treating the light-hearted like they are not smart. Know that you *are* smart. You are probably very intuitive and sincere. These are the qualities that you need to fix up. If we all espoused them, the world would be a very different place to live in.

K – Keep learning, evolving and changing

Update like a champion – look for challenges and opportunities.

Why do we need to continue to update our lives? A lifetime of learning can keep both the body and mind active. Most people think learning just takes place in educational environments, on courses or from people that have already done it, but life is a continuous update and there are so many people and platforms available that you could learn from.

Research has suggested that continued cognitive activity has a positive effect on brain cells and helps promote mental sharpness. The subject may be academic in nature or it may have more personal significance, for example learning about your culture or tracing your family roots.

Physically, lifelong learning can entail taking exercise or dance classes, learning how to swim or even picking up a new sport. Continuous updating enriches your life with the things that will spark your curiosity because you want to know *how*, *what* or *why*.

Taking up a class or hobby can be a social activity as well as an educational one. You can make friends with different interests and get involved with the communities you care about, curbing loneliness and stress. And your hobby may bring opportunities for travel, giving you a chance to see more of the world, to experience life in another culture and to gain perspective on your own.

You do not need to be enrolled in a formal degree programme to develop your own interests. In the last couple of years, I have updated myself through a weird and wonderful range of courses and opportunities, including becoming a GB archery coach, becoming a mental first aider , donating blood over fifty times, getting on a BBC TV game show, entering the FA People's Cup, attending cookery courses, presenting on radio, opening tea shops around the country and even creating my own podcast. All these new updates have positively contributed to my own personal development and helped me develop a lighter mind.

Look up for the new update

Research has indicated that millennials prioritise *happiness* and *learning* because they see the connection between the two. This is true for any age, but younger people have embraced technology and become more connected because of it. Millennials are travelling the world, learning a second language and more. They are the happiest generation at work, and part of this is due to their desire for continuous learning opportunities, at work as well as in their personal lives.

You need to evaluate your current situation and ask yourself: when was your last new update, something that took you out of your comfort zone? We are a species of habit; we like going to the same places to eat, or even enjoying the same holiday destination. It makes the choice simpler, but it does not encourage our state of mind to grow or develop. *Continuous learning* is a constant state of acquiring new knowledge, skills and tools to support our organisational goals, and is thus a cornerstone of life and evolution.

So what is your current state? If it's constant with no new updates planned, just more of the same old memories and experiences that feel empty and soulless, then it's time to change your state as this is only temporary.

There are two states of mind with regard to change: *change is constant* or *change is a constant*. Both of these sound correct, and may even sound the same, but there is a huge difference in the meaning – just one that is hard to articulate.

Change is constant is an adjective, meaning that change is occurring continuously, while *change is a constant* is a noun, meaning that change is an always-to-be-expected condition. So you're asking, what are the differences? Let's apply it to a real situation so you can gain a better understanding.

Both situations use similar processes, but the outcomes are very different. Consider Adrian, who is always following other people's lives, so he is continually updating his wardrobe and chasing that next holiday destination on his Instagram feed. By topping up his tan and going to different places, it seems that he is updating continuously; but the real story is that he relies on the same brands and shops for his new wardrobe, and he always goes on all-inclusive holidays. So the change is constant (adjective) but there is no personal development or growth.

Dawn expects change (noun) too as he grows. He is always looking for a wardrobe update and roams different shops and brands to find something new for himself. His holidays involve strange locations, strange accommodations and even stranger activities to experience; he never pre-books and always goes with the most difficult option. He conditions himself to accept that life's greatest lessons are usually learnt at the worst times, so change becomes an expected condition that will inevitably bring some pain and suffering.

Light up your update

Having a dedicated daily plan can be great, but it can also get dull – and a bored mind isn't one that's gaining intelligence or growth, I can tell you that much. Updating trains your brain into thinking more creatively about your life.

Try a new food, listen to that new music artist, and abandon your Sunday errands. You can stick to your preferences, but venturing out and mixing up how you do things and the order in which you do them may have a powerful impact on your mindset and, consequently, the way in which you contribute to the learning process. The greatest learning takes place via collaboration and in communities, because as a divergent learner you need to adapt to a wide range of mindsets and thinking. Explore different topics and don't be afraid to ask for clarity. Be inquisitive, and if your intent is sincere, there will be people who will help and support you in your journey.

Fix up your update

When it comes down to it, first you need to stop the constant which is the old update, the old habit. *Try something new* is a good start to your learning process: a new restaurant, a new supermarket, a different type of holiday. Something that will make people around you surprised is a good start, as that will demonstrate a *real* shift in the mindset.

How does Dawn see learning? To him, it is a continuous process of improvement and progress through absorbing, processing and retaining knowledge – and failing is part of it.

Check out one new podcast this week. Try a new restaurant or cuisine. Try watching something new on YouTube, or read a book from someone you don't really admire. Try to find the answer to one new thing a day. If you find it, awesome. If that satisfies your curiosity, move on. But if you dig deeper and find more interesting questions, then you just might be on your way to adding a new interest to your life. Never stop the updates and keep exercising that brain of yours.

Experiment with the updates. Keep the momentum going. Keep learning, and make sure change is always the expected condition. If you truly live by this mindset, life will never be the same. I mean that: life will *never* be the same.

Update Eight
Look up to the STARS

N ow let's focus on the remaining five rays of the ten that make up the wheel of light. It's time to turn our attention to the STARS.

| Space | Time | Actions | Real bonds | Self care |

S – Space

Most of the universe is empty space, called a vacuum, but it is an imperfect vacuum like our lives. There are clouds of interstellar dust, and the tiny particles that make up the solar wind. Meanwhile, electromagnetic radiation such as radio, heat (infrared) and X-rays all echo through space, as do the beams of light that create and sustain life.

The universe is all of space and time and their contents, including planets, stars, galaxies, and all other forms of matter and energy. The largest-scale objects, the galaxies, are distributed uniformly in all directions, meaning that the universe has neither a centre nor an edge; it is limitless, just like our potential.

Our own space is very important to how we see the world and how we behave in that environment. The dust and tiny particles are the clutter in both your mind and environment that was mentioned in Update Four.

Look up

What is our *space*? Objects and events have relative position and direction, so how does that apply to us? What is the physical environment you spend your time in; does that space inspire you to live the way you want? Does your home, workplace or your social environment excite and enliven you?

The entrance to your home is most important as it's the first and last thing you see when you enter and leave. Does it provide a welcoming, secure environment, establishing the capability for happiness and growth? Does your home create an environment that will maximise the incubation of happiness? Is it flexible, to accommodate both current and evolving behaviours; is it future-proofed to enable the space to be reallocated and reconfigured; creative, to energise and inspire everyone that occupies that space; supportive, to develop the potential of all learners; and lastly, enterprising to make the space capable of supporting different purposes and occasions? The first step is to declutter as mentioned earlier in the book.

Light up: live in colour

Here's how you could plan to make your home space lighter with four simple steps:

1. **Improve your home's traffic flow**

   How you and guests move through your space has a big effect on how spacious your home is perceived to be. If you've never evaluated how traffic moves through your space, take a few minutes to move through your house, from room to room and *in* each room.

2. **Rearrange with the goal to balance the light**

   The idea behind this is to move the 'heaviness' away from the entry of each room and/or spread the weight equally around the room. So instead of having the first thing you see in a space be a heavy piece of furniture, make it something visually light, low or even just space. By dispersing the weight of a room equally, you'll keep your eye moving throughout a room. Don't be afraid to rearrange furniture from room to room to achieve better balanced Zen space.

3. **Clear spaces to simplify – align the light**

   In small spaces, the clutter you keep on your counters and in full view should be the things you access daily. If you keep the toaster out on the counter but you only use it once a month, it's just not helping anybody, and it's not that big a deal to get it out when you do use it.

Is there room for it in a cabinet somewhere? But that's just one example; the idea could apply to bathroom toiletries you don't use every day, or even to bigger items like extra seating. Yes, storage may be tight, but get creative. Declutter your current storage and maximise shelving for more room and light up your space.

4. **Bring in the light**

See if the space could benefit from a window being decluttered. Depending on your type of window, if you take off window coverings altogether, it could give the space a more architectural feel, and it'll certainly let in more natural light. There's no rule dictating that your home can't be colourful.

Fix up

Once you have fixed your home space, you can focus on the other spaces that will lighten up your life, such as your work or social spaces. Staying disciplined and focused in your spaces is extremely important as these are the environments that you will grow into.

T – Time management

Time management is the ability to plan and control how you spend the hours in a day to effectively accomplish your goals. This involves balancing time between the different elements of work, home, social life and health. It is important to establish clear goals and priorities in order to set aside non-essential tasks that can eat up time, and to monitor where the time goes. Good time management requires an important shift in mindset from tasks/activities to results/actions.

Look up

Being busy isn't the same as being effective. Spending your day in a frenzy of activity often achieves less, because you're dividing your attention between so many different tasks. Good time management lets you work smarter, not harder, so you get more done in less time. Poor time management can be related to buffering, attention problems, or difficulties with self-control.

Light up

Everyone has the same amount of time in one day and that is 86,400 seconds, or 1,440 minutes; but how we use that time, and what we would like to achieve from our day, will differ from individual to individual.

First we need to turn a deaf ear: we all refuse to listen to our own conscious when we forget to get things done or we just can't remember. Our brains are made for creativity, not for storing, so how do we plan our day on a daily, weekly, monthly and yearly basis?

Fix up: be DEAF

So how do you use the DEAF model to manage your day?
- Define your lifestyle and plan your time.
- Eliminate the clutter: stop, reset and restart.
- Auto-correct: Plan, organise and action.
- Freedom: Do what you want to do.

The saying 'work smarter, not harder' has become a staple in the way I go about work of any kind. Instead of being robotic and repetitive in how you approach tasks, try to be thoughtful and always ask yourself if something can be done more efficiently, or eliminated altogether. Managing your time isn't about squeezing as many tasks into your day as possible: it's about simplifying how you work, achieving goals faster, and relieving and managing stress levels. Control what you ***can*** control.

A – Actions to live & earn

Buy what you need, and you will get the life that you want.

How do you ensure that you are taking the right actions so that you have enough finance not only to provide for your current needs, but also to make your future better? If I want to get an idea of your desire to grow and develop, I ask a simple question:

Are you satisfied with your actions right now?

Look up

If the answer is, 'I'm very satisfied, very content with where I am,' I conclude that there is very little potential for future growth. Being content is one part of life's equation for happiness; but when contentment is used as a tool to 'cap off' personal growth, it becomes harmful. Personal desire is the first key to personal growth: your desire to change, evolve and update.

Whenever you learn, feel or know something, desire was already there waiting. It's the vehicle that carries you where you need to go. I would love to shine a light for some people, but I soon discover that I've run out of batteries! They're not going anywhere, and that's fine: it's their choice. I'm not responsible for something over which I have no control. It's okay, and I'll love them where they are.

When you have a lighter mind, you still have passion. You still have desires. I'm not all that I want to be, nor have I accomplished all that I want to accomplish. That fire within you is called desire: the desire to make your life count by making a difference.

Purchasing decisions are made subconsciously, so that means we're not deciding logically; we're relying on our emotions. Adverts that tell stories are always more compelling than lists of features. Why? Because they play with our emotions. Stories activate our subconscious, making us feel more worthless and penniless.

At the same time, society is shifting. In the past, possessions and status symbols like the corner office were a big deal, but now people crave *experiences*. The value of experiences is so powerful in the consumer world that it's created new business models. The sharing economy and the boom in subscription services are two examples. In both situations, you can get everything you need without owning anything. For example, most of us now stream our music without purchasing a single song. And social media focuses on pictures, stories, and videos about what people are *doing* right at that moment, instead of what they own long-term.

Light up

I have the privilege of spending time with a lot of people that have lived their life happily, and I always ask them the same question: how do you stay so enthusiastic and passionate about life and how do you sustain happiness? Some of their answers include:

- 'The day your past becomes more exciting than your future is the day you start to die.'
- 'In the end you only regret the chances you didn't take.'
- 'Enjoy your life and don't compare.'
- 'I wish I spent more time at home.'
- 'Your last breath should be your best version of yourself.'

So to keep the desire burning bright, take actions that will get you out of the comfort zone. Contentment and satisfaction are good things, but they were never intended to create the ideal conditions for happiness. At times, the lights of desire glow dim on our journey of life; these are the times when you keep the light burning. Eventually you will see your desire move you forward.

Napoleon Hill said, 'The starting point of all achievement is desire.' Weak desires bring weak results. Just as weak fires leave us a little cold. And they're not much to look at either.

Fix up

While you're updating, think **big**! You can always act small later. The real danger starts by putting limitations on your thinking and choosing the default option.

In our attempt to be practical, we often play it too safe. Use the following questions to help break the updating glitch:

- What are the things you would like to do well?
- What are the experiences you would like to have?
- What do you want to start doing right now?
- What are three non-negotiable values in your life?
- What things, events or activities make you feel fully alive?
- What have you let slide? Why? What can you do now to reverse that?

R – Real bonds

'So much learning yet nobody taught me to be loved.'

A *real bond* is one where the love is not a result of need. Most of the time we care for someone because we need to. Real bonds get us out of our selfish behaviour and allow us to care for that person irrespective of how they make us feel; it's not an exchange process, more one of giving value and creating opportunities to grow.

Look up

Humans are inherently social animals, who are happier and healthier when connected to others and creating bonds. Feeling isolated and lonely, in contrast, is a stress factor that poses a health risk comparable to smoking and obesity. Having positive social bonds is a key ingredient for happiness.

Where do we find different types of real bonds? We don't have to look far. Living things are made up of atoms, but in most cases those atoms aren't just floating around individually. Instead, they're usually interacting with other atoms (or groups of atoms), just like the way society works in our daily life.

For instance, atoms might be connected by strong bonds and organised into molecules; or they might form temporary, weak bonds with other atoms that they bump into or brush up against. Both the strong bonds that hold molecules together and the weaker bonds that create temporary connections are essential to the chemistry of our bodies, and to the existence of life itself. Does this sound like the way that people construct bonds in our human society?

Why do chemical bonds, and real relationship bonds, form? The basic answer is that atoms are trying to reach the most stable (lowest energy) state that they can; and humans are trying to create a similar state, which could be called contentment – and we are happy when we are loved. For example, Dawn is looking to gain new relationships with new people that will create a more stable and mean-ingful state of mind for himself, maybe a new circle of friends with new positive interests or people with different minds; but he may need to lose a few people on the way to make space and time for the new bonds.

Light up

Consider these questions before you update:

- Are you going to reconnect? (new bonds)
- What new connections would you like to update? (energy growth bonds)
- Are you going to disconnect with someone that drains your energy? (weak/strong organic bonds)

New bonds

An atom consists of a positively charged nucleus orbited by *electrons*, which have a negative charge. In its default state, the two balance out so that overall the atom has no net electric charge; but an atom can lose or gain one or more electrons to form what is called an *ion*. The loss of an electron results in a positive ion (*cation*), while gaining an electron creates a negative ion (*anion*). When one atom loses an electron and another atom gains that electron, the process is called *electron transfer*.

For example, suppose Jack (from *Jack and the Beanstalk*) has a bag of magic beans and he gives one of them away to someone that has a greater need, and then he helps to nurture that bean with his own water and light energy. He has not just grown a beanstalk for someone else, but now he may be in a better position to nurture his own.

This could also be applied to parenting, as creating a new bond with your new child may require you to give up some of your current bonds with friends and family, or even your own partner.

In general, the loss of an electron by one atom and its gain by another must happen at the same time for the exchange not to lose energy, and that is the problem for us too when new bonds are created: old ones can be neglected, and the energy in those old bonds can be lost. The key is that both bonds, old and new, need equal investment with time and energy so that there is no energy loss and both bonds can stay strong. If there is an energy imbalance, someone will be neglected.

Energy growth bonds

Certain ions are necessary in the body for nerve impulse conduction, muscle contractions, water balance and other functions. Many sports drinks and dietary supplements provide these ions to replace those lost from the body via sweating during exercise.

Ionic bonds are bonds formed between ions with opposite charges. With people, too, it's often said that opposites attract, and this theory supports that. Do we create bonds with people who have a different mindset, a different energy, from ourselves? For example, does Adrian have friends from different walks of life, social groups, jobs and interests, or do they just mirror his behaviours and actions? This is Dawn's strength, as he has a range of relationships with different types of people who have a wide variety of mindsets and views. Having different bonds will expand your perspective.

Another way atoms can become more stable is by sharing electrons (rather than fully gaining or losing them), thus forming *covalent bonds*. The more electrons that are shared between two atoms, the stronger their bond will be. This is a good example of networking and collaboration; growing together will always create a stronger bond as you are sharing your energy and resources for communal growth. Working in a group or team will always be better than working on your own.

There are two basic types of covalent bonds: polar and nonpolar. In a *polar bond*, the electrons are unequally shared by the atoms and spend more time close to one atom than the other, because of the unequal distribution of electrons between the atoms of different elements. Let's apply this to Adrian who has just started a new relationship with someone he has met at work. He used to meet his work friends for lunch and play football every Wednesday night; but once this new relationship started, the imbalance in time and energy began as he stopped going out for lunches and stopped playing football that he enjoyed. His key priority was just to create a strong bond with his new girlfriend, but at the same time this meant sacrificing other bonds.

Nonpolar covalent bonds form between two atoms of the same element, or between atoms of different elements that share electrons more or less equally. This principle is again mirrored in real bonds between people, when the energy and resources are equally distributed. Dawn has just started a new job and wants to create real strong bonds with his new work colleagues; but he is still not neglecting the other important bonds in his life, such as those with his family and friends. So we see that Adrian has very strong bonds with a small group of people with similar mindsets, whereas Dawn has temporary bonds with a large group of different people and can choose when to make those bonds stronger depending on his priorities.

Where do you stand on your relationships and your bonds?

Weak and strong bonds

Both strong and weak bonds play key roles in the chemistry of our cells and bodies as well as in our relationships.

 For instance, strong bonds hold together the chemical building blocks that make up a strand of DNA. However, weaker hydrogen bonds hold together the two strands of the DNA double helix.

We should be continually creating new bonds every day, from the barista at a coffee shop to colleagues at work; but how do we create long-lasting relationships? The answer is that you can't. What's amazing is to think that billions of these chemical bond interactions – strong and weak, stable and temporary – are going on in our bodies right now, holding us together and keeping us ticking. But none of these bonds are permanent, as they are ever changing and evolving.

Fix up

Therefore, the secret of creating meaningful and real bonds in your life is to accept that no relationship is strong, permanent and stable; they are all temporary, as in real bonds dynamics, values, interests, independence and confidence all grow and develop.

Real bonds are when *all* your relationships are growing in different directions and at different speeds, and your light mind is continuously being updated. Relationships change, evolve and some will be lost.

I hope you have a better understanding of relationships and are able to reflect on your circle of influence and whether you need to change or move on. It's now time to find your social connections that will create the best conditions for you to grow.

S – Self-care and mindfulness

This section is all about your mental happiness and how your consciousness can cope with the everyday stresses that life brings us.

What is mental health? The World Health Organisation defines it as 'a state of well-being in which an individual realises his or her own abilities, can cope with the normal stresses of life, can work productively and is able to make a contribution to his or her community'.

Look up

A person with good mental health will feel in control of their emotions, have a light mindset and experience positive interactions with people around them, but for many people in the real world this is not the case. To some degree, we all experience mental illness that stops us from having control. Most people have multiple episodes of illness and periods of wellness in between; only a small minority have ongoing mental health issues. Furthermore, women usually experience more anxiety and mood disorders than men, while men tend to have more issues related to substance use.

Society does not really understand mental illness, and it can be seen as being lost in the darkness; so recovery can be a long process, often described as a journey, and it may not necessarily be a linear one. There will be many dark days ahead. Mental ill-health affects people differently, and the journey of recovery will be different for each person.

Recovery encompasses the lived experiences of people as they accept and overcome the challenge of their mental health issue. It provides an empowering message of hope, which says that, regardless of symptoms, people should have every opportunity to lead fulfilled and satisfying lives. Recovery is a deeply personal process, but people don't recover in isolation: they need support and hope. This means that mental health is everyone's business; the attitudes and beliefs that society holds about mental illness and well-being have a powerful impact on someone's experiences and their recovery.

Light up

20/20 is a term I use to describe our individual vision of the world, based on the 20/20 concept of normal vision or perfect eyesight. What this means is that, to make sense of the world around us, we need to be able to see it without filters and with clear vision.

 We are all shaped by our past experiences and beliefs, but we all see things slightly differently, and consequently we treat ourselves and other people differently, too. Our 20/20 vision is influenced by a range of factors that stem from our upbringing and experience.

The chart below asks you to consider how you see these 20 factors that may have moulded your beliefs. Mark with a tick how you see each factor and how much of an influence it has had on your beliefs. Is it significant or not significant?

This process, and the understanding you gain from it, should support you in making your journey ahead clearer and help you with the updates to come.

	Significant in life	Not significant in life
Age		
Aspirations		
Background		
Chronic illness		
Cultural forces		
Disability		
Learnings		
Family environment		
Gender		
Interests/Hobbies		
Likes/Dislikes		
Mental health		
Past achievements		
Relationships		
Status		
Sexuality		
Social media identity		
Spirituality		
Values		
Work/Education		

● ● ● ● ○

People become ill when the stress they face becomes more than they can cope with. Our vulnerability to stress and our ability to deal with it varies, so problems that one person may take in their stride might be enough to cause another person to become depressed or develop mental illness. Evidence suggests that some of this is linked to genetics, but coping styles and mindsets are very important as well.

Consider how Dawn and Adrian will deal with the same situation but in different ways. Their social skills and environment contribute too. They are both going on their first holiday abroad. This is always a stressful situation for everyone; it's not the holiday that is stressful but more the first-time experience, as it's the fear of the unknown.

Dawn has chosen to stay in on Friday night to research the country that he is visiting. He downloaded a language app and bought a map for the city; he even invited a friend around for advice regarding his concerns. His stress levels have reduced as he is feeling more confident about the trip now. Meanwhile, Adrian has chosen to still meet friends for a night out, and doesn't have the confidence to talk about his holiday. He hasn't packed his bag yet, and has had no time to research as he has delayed dealing with the situation, so his stress levels have increased.

One of the most common contributors to mental ill-health is depression. Everyone can feel in a dark place sometimes which may be a short-term depressed mood, but most manage to cope and soon recover without treatment. More worrying is what is called *clinical depression*; that is, one that lasts for at least two weeks and which affects the person's behaviour and has physical, emotional and cognitive effects. It also interferes with the ability to function at work and to have satisfying relationships.

A person experiencing depression commonly has a dark view of themselves, the world and the future. Their thoughts often follow themes of hopelessness and helplessness. In worse cases this could lead to suicide, but it can be preventable; most suicidal people don't want to die, they simply don't want to live with the pain or darkness any longer.

Another misunderstanding is the belief that addiction and substance misuse are the same, whereas in fact they relate to different emotions. Substance misuse is when a person is using alcohol or other drugs for a period and becomes physically or psychologically dependent on them. Substance misuse is not just a matter of how much of the substance a person uses, but how its use affects their life and the lives of those around them. It is a simple process of self-harming during which the mind becomes darker.

Addiction is the opposite of connection, as the mind becomes fearful of the unknown and of making new connections for change. Instead, the mind would rather update through compulsive engagement with something predictable and reliable, such as gambling, alcohol, drugs or even work. Some people use alcohol to reduce anxiety and to relax and feel more extroverted, but it may lead to them feeling more aggressive and prone to risk-taking.

Mental resilience and recovery can also be about growth. Recovery requires growing new skills to support mental well-being, along with growing new and existing relationships to provide support at times of difficulty. It represents a flourishing of values and beliefs that allow the person to define themselves beyond ideas of illness and disease.

Hope, too, is central to recovery. Create seeds of hope that can be cultivated and grown: the hope that someone who may be struggling with difficult experience can feel accepted and understood, and become connected to their own internal capacity for self-reflection and greater resilience through self-help.

Fix up

Starting the conversation about your feelings is the first step on the road to improving your mental health. The state of your mental health is not permanent, as people experience traumas and stress at different stages of their lives but respond in diverse ways. This could be a positive or negative trigger for you and your mental health.

Stress is everywhere, and it is directly linked to our mental health. At any one time, one in six adults in Britain will be experiencing depression, anxiety or other problems related to stress. By tackling stress, we can go a long way to tackle mental health problems such as anxiety, depression and, in some instances, self-harm and suicide. Understanding what causes us stress and taking action to manage our stress levels is a key part of looking after our well-being and happiness.

● ● ● ● ●

Consider how CRACK and STARS affect your personal updates.

The biggest challenge in all of this is getting the right balance; in fact, the truth is, it's impossible. So giving the right amount of attention to each ray of light at the right time, prioritising each of the different updates at different times, will help you embrace the *imbalance* in your life. True happiness is found in the imbalance. A happy life isn't about doing everything, it's about enjoying everything.

Update Nine
Find your light, find your DASH

F INDING YOUR PURPOSE is like finding the fire that will burn down your limitations. It's the light that shows you the path when life gets dark. Your purpose will be your guide in all of life's big decisions; it will influence your behaviour, shape your goals, offer a sense of direction, and create meaning to your life.

Like so many others I have struggled with this concept all my life; but during the process of developing a lighter mindset I realised that the concept was flawed, as I was always searching for what I could do with my life, always looking for meaning and significance. As I have become more self-aware, and through the process of continuously reflecting, I have realised that the answer was in my behaviours, and that my true purpose lay along the path of service and support for others.

You have found true purpose when the light you emit is more than the light you absorb. What does that mean? You are self-aware of your decisions and behaviours, so you are able to support and help others. The combined value and performance of two identities will be greater than the sum of the separate individual parts; this concept is known as *synergy*.

Your purpose is greater than you alone. True happiness does not come from within but from how we are connected to the environment around us; it comes from family, friends and other social groups that we are connected with and how we can influence and support them to grow.

● ● ● ● ●

I discovered something that helped me identify my purpose when I had a chance to visit graveyards for a research project. I was conditioned to count the number of years each person had lived, but quickly I realised that this was not important. It's not about how long you live in the world, but more about what you do while you are present in the world: the dash ('–') between the date when you were born and the date you die. Everyone's life has a start and finish date, but the dash is the important part as it represents what you have achieved in between.

The formula below will help focus your mindset on the key elements of DASH, which represents your essence and your:

<u>D</u>NA
<u>A</u>ims and purpose
<u>S</u>uccess
<u>H</u>appiness

D – DNA

What is your DNA? What makes you?

How do you know whether you are shining the light on the right path? You need to consider your own core values: these are guiding principles that dictate behaviour and can help you understand the difference between right and wrong. Your DNA can also help you to determine if you are on the right path and fulfilling your own goals by creating an unwavering guide.

How do we determine what are our values, and how many principles do we need? Consider this: there are only **three** primary colours (red, yellow and blue) needed to mix all other colours. Three is the number for time: past, present and future, and also birth, life and death.

The Borromean rings on the left are three rings that are interlocked, yet if any single ring is removed the other two will fall apart. This is a little like your core values. Spend time on what makes you; what is your real essence, and what makes you, **you**. Write down all your values, but try to narrow it down to three core values that you live by every day.

A – Aim, purpose, pain and passion

We all aim to achieve something in life and have a true purpose and passion that will guide life decisions, influence behaviour, shape goals and give meaning to our lives. The ideal we aspire to is to live a life full of passion: one where we never feel bored or stagnant, we're constantly excited and inspired and never feel lonely or worthless. But there are many ways to live life – there is no right or wrong.

Some questions that will lighten the mind on this subject:

1. What is the aim of your life?
2. What are your goals? Remember these are your **own** goals, not society's metrics.
3. Why do you do what you do? The bigger the *why*, the greater the purpose.
4. Is the *why* greater than being just about you?
5. How much pain and hard work are you willing to endure to achieve your goals?
6. What would you do if money was no object?

True purpose comes from something bigger than yourself, while passion grows from within; but passion and purpose are connected by the element of *pain*. Without passion life seems meaningless and mundane; so the question is, how much pain are you willing to experience to live your life of passion and purpose?

S – Success

Success means something different to every single person, so you need to create your own definition. The dark mind suggests that success is the external value of yourself judged according to the metrics that you have absorbed from others. That could be wealth, body shape, number of followers or even the concept of being famous.

Adrian sees success as a product, something tangible that could be reached, and his mind is wired to consume and chase other people's successes. He is scrolling to look for other people's definition of success and make it his own. Dawn, on the other hand, sees success as having autonomy and freedom; the light mind suggests that success is a journey, not a destination.

The rays of light defined in Updates Seven and Eight outline the key areas where you could succeed in your life. The wheel of light is a way to take a good hard look at each element of your life and rate its relative quality level, so you can uncover which areas need more attention than others. As I said in the introduction to Update Seven, you need a selective approach rather than a full range of actions.

Because success is subjective, there can be no single definition that works for everyone, but perhaps success can be described as living your best life and becoming the best version of yourself.

You need to create your own metrics for success that work for you. If success were measured and valued only on your own metrics, would everyone be happy?

H – Happiness

Happiness is used in the context of mental or emotional states; it may be a feeling, or it could be a mindset. We are all looking for this state or feeling.

Aristotle said: 'Happiness is the meaning and the purpose of life, the whole aim and end of human existence.'

I think we must look at that quote from a different mindset, because it seems to imply that happiness is the main goal; but happiness can't be a goal in itself. It's not something that's achievable, or pursued, or even bought. I believe that happiness is merely a by-product of usefulness to society: making a difference in the world and adding value to the present. By simply leaving the world better than you found it, you create your own mental happiness.

Most things we do in life are just dark moments and experiences, as we pursue happiness:

- We consume
- We buy
- We sell

Those things should make you happy, right? But they are not useful. You are not creating anything of value. You're just consuming; it's not what gives meaning to life.

What really makes your mind happy is when you are useful: when you discover a solution that others can use, or create something that will make people's lives better. For a long time I found it difficult to explain the concept of usefulness and happiness, but the activities below highlight the true meaning:

- We think
- We give
- We create
- We serve
- We reflect
- We change

You don't find happiness, you can't consume happiness, you must create it. There is no end to the process of happiness as everything keeps updating: the world, your mind, and even society. The solution is to manage and control your mind continuum and focus on the elements that will make you happier.

Upgrade your mind

The key updates are the process, and the upgrade is the outcome. The upgrade symbol on the right is the Japanese word *kaizen*, which means 'change for better' and also means continuous improvement. It  represents improvement of your mind and your life, every day, everybody and everywhere.

Stop searching and start the process of grinding, working, hustling and questioning whether the new update is worth the pain and suffering. The upgrade is a lighter mindset where you can rethink problems, creating better solutions to experience happier outcomes. Change must be the upgrade; it is not a habit but a condition, and change is constant. It needs to be compounded like interest: build on every little improvement with your **M**indset, **A**ctions and **D**ecisions – time to go MAD and behave in an unreasonable way. Change is difficult, as it will be painful for you and everyone around you.

It's time to upgrade and be the best version of yourself. In a way it is similar to playing a video game. Each level you play improves your skills, and you move up to the next level once you've conquered a certain stage. You could find shortcuts and cheats to get to the next level, but that is only cheating yourself; upgrading takes time and patience. The levels are infinite, so the personal growth is limitless too; the challenge is to be disciplined to improve every day, everywhere and everything.

The upgrade process involves decoding your problems to find the solutions best suited to yourself; unlocking your mind to take the actions and search for the solutions that will make a better *you*. Unleash your potential to your unlimited power, find your frequency and then create consistency. The upgrade can easily be misinterpreted as external value: for example, moving to an affluent area but not focusing on your intellect and refinement, or fitting a new kitchen and not upgrading your cookery skills.

The upgrade will be frightening, but the aim is to be better than the person that you were yesterday. You don't have to compare yourself with others; this is your own upgrade, you own it and you can upgrade at whatever pace you want as long as you are making progress and having fun. The update can be something small or big as long as you control the update and your pendulum is swinging continuously.

To reboot and restart your mind continuum you must control three elements in your life: your mindset, your imagination, and the actions you take to create an alternative reality.

REBOOT = Mindset + Imagination – Reality

I hope you now have the courage to take your mind to the next level and start your upgrade by managing your mindset from dark to light, altering your imagination by reducing the buffering, and deleting the current reality and updating your frequency to an alternative one.

Update differently

Energy can be neither created nor destroyed; energy can only be transferred, or changed from one form to another, from dark to light or light to dark. If you focus your energy on the pain and suffering, the pain will get greater; but if you focus your energy on hope and faith, that will flourish. The secret is to find your personal frequency and keep the energy moving. Every update and experience is energy that enters your body, but the mind will lighten or darken depending on your energy and your focus.

When I started this book, I interviewed many successful millionaires and people who had climbed to the top of the corporate ladder. In my naive state of learning, I thought they were focused on being the best version of themselves; but when I dived deeper into the lives of society's so-called game-changers, I realised a lot of them had gained notoriety by sacrificing areas that were more important long-term. A woman who became a VP in a bank, but never saw her kids and her husband during the week, became a daytime alcoholic. A man who built a property empire worth millions spent most nights cheating on his wife. As I talked to more people, a pattern emerged: some of them were sacrificing their long-term happiness for short-term success.

My current definition of a *real* game-changer is someone who plays their own game and focuses their energy on the important long game of being the best possible version of themself. It requires everyday, everybody and everywhere improvement of your mind and your life. Consider the greatest contribution you can make to the world and to the people around you whom you love. If you channel and direct your own energy, you can live a life full of abundance and happiness so you can better serve others.

● ● ● ● ●

I hope you can *start* your story of true commitment by updating differently for your happiness. Be inspired to live for happiness and make it your only star; keep orbiting till you discover your happiness. Keep searching the universe for the answers. Don't be distracted by the flashy lights of other stars or the fear of not shining bright. There is *one* sun that gives us life; without it we would not exist.

It's time to become who you want to be and create that alternative reality that you truly deserve; swing the pendulum and be the master of your destiny. The only fear is not being happy; unhappiness is a lonely place. Start to make the changes, as things can never be the same. Ready or not, take the shackles off and update your happiness. Life should now be like a new set of rules for the way you want to live. Happiness must be created by you; as Gandhi said, 'Be the change you want to see in the world.'

Yes, life is constantly presenting us with challenges and opportunities to grow, learn and be more than we currently are – often long before we are ready. Life is a game. Your relationship with your *ego* is very important during this game, as it can turn into either an enemy or an ally. The ego causes most of your suffering, but it can also save you from further pain. Time for your ego to blow away the gremlins and start a new game – or maybe you need to stop repeating your own game again and again and start sharing the game with others. Instead of pretending that you have mastered your game, remain focused on the updating – and updating differently by playing a better version of your own game. Saying *no* may protect you from improving your game, but it's actually the most effective barrier to success, so make *yes* your preferred option or behaviour. *Yes* to your own personal growth and development. *Yes* to a better version of yourself, *yes* to self-love and self-development. *Yes* it is hard, *yes* sometimes it will not work. *Yes* it will be out of my comfort zone.

When people ask me the question 'Are you happy?', I always ask myself, how do I prove it and how do I prove that I am getting happier? I have concluded that it is easier to prove over time than it is to capture it in a moment. Consider these two mindsets with two stories on becoming fitter. Adrian chooses to attend a two-day boot camp and, when he arrives back from the weekend, he looks in the mirror to see if there has been any change; but he doesn't see it, and so he gives up on becoming fitter. In contrast, Dawn exercises for 20 minutes a day over a six-month period. He too looks in the mirror every day for 180 days straight; he does not notice a change from one day to the next, but over time he sees that he is progressing. The importance of upgrading is not about the intensity but about consistency. You need to commit to the **habit** of upgrading, and ensuring your pendulum keeps moving consistently; take ownership of your own swing.

Dawn has chosen to start walking to work twice a week rather than take the car. He listens to music that he enjoys, and he uses the money he saves on fuel to buy e-books for himself to read at weekends. This one small change has made him aware that both his mental and physical health have improved, and that in turn has created other upgrades in his life.

The greatest challenge is having the courage to start the first update and make it a reality. If not, the dark mind will start to buffer and download all the useless information that will fuel your imagination and block out the reality of the way forward. You will end up downloading and consuming updates that will make the possible into the impossible; your dark past experiences will support the theories of what you can lose rather than what you can gain. Reality will certainly reduce the fear; doing something will certainly help. Take control of your future today.

● ● ● ● ●

It's time for you to centre your thoughts and reflect on the decluttering process that will unlock the mind, search for your own light, prioritise your CRACK and STARS and create awareness of your DASH with all the new updates. Use your conscious intentions to manifest your happiness and create your own light that will shine bright. For every problem, you will seek a creative solution; in every failure you will find success; and, when life becomes comfortable, you will shift the frequency. You now possess the tools and strategies to manage your mind.

| Connect | Reckless | Active | Care | Keep learning |

| Space | Time | Actions | Real bonds | Self care |

You now have the key to using all the energy and potential within you to create your own happiness and design the life that you deserve to live with true enlightenment.

● ● ● ● ●

I'm sure you've said to yourself on occasion (or maybe all the damn time) that you need to make changes in your life, especially when the world shut down due to Covid-19 and we were all isolated and looking for the next update. You might have felt stuck where you are with no sense of fulfilment in your life. When it comes down to it, we all want to feel fulfilled in our work, our personal lives, and our relationships. If we start to act with more intention, we create the foundation needed to **make** changes in our lives instead of just wishing for them.

You can design your life in any way that you want to. You just need to be clear and committed to your idea. There's no point updating when it does not lead to an up-grade that adds value to your happiness; a high-frequency update like going to the Maldives with a broken marriage, or buying dumb shit to impress others, will only make your mind unhappy. The true update needs to create value for your mind to upgrade, so that you feel happier and able to be better for **you**.

In the process of searching for happiness, I actually discovered what type of mind creates unhappiness. An unhappy mind is one that keeps using the same solutions when life has the same problems, but there is no progress or upgrade; the mind is not willing to change when any new updates become available. Instead, it shuts down; life is the same, but time moves on, like Groundhog Day. The mind tries to improve and update, but it may not realise that time has outpaced it, so any new update of knowledge or understanding will be logged off as the mind feels dis-connected from the new reality. Any goals or expectations that it may create will be silenced; the possible becomes the impossible as the mind settles for the destination that is the most comfortable. Happiness becomes a default setting based on what you were going to **be** rather than what you can **become**. The unhappy mind settles for a low and consistent frequency between the light and dark – the comfort zone. It will not take on any problems, and will avoid any suffering and pain connected with new solutions. The frequency and consistency will be limited on the mind continuum as the thought processes are fixed, and therefore personal growth is stagnated. Failure becomes the only limiting factor to the mind's potential.

	LIGHT	UNHAPPY MIND	DARK
LIFE		Shut down	
INTELLIGENCE		Logged off	
GOALS		Silent	
HAPPINESS		Default	
THINKING		Fixed	

I hope this book has given you some inspiration to live your life more intentionally. Remember that you get to design your happiness in any way you want to – you just have to be committed to your mind's development. The purpose of this book is to inspire you to think differently and be the future solution-makers to light the way for a better tomorrow.

Be better and upgrade to the best version you can be. You can now take your mind to the next level, and accept that the change will create a better *you*. We all experience the feeling of not really knowing what we want, constantly second-guessing ourselves. Is this job right for me? Am I in the right relationship? What if I am meant to be doing something else?

Having fun during the process can change this quickly. Passion and purpose are easily achieved by merely discovering your own consistent frequency. At the same time, your perception will change – because the changes that matter most are often changes of perception rather than changes in the world around us. By asking yourself the right questions in the right way, you build your own light-mind continuum and *become* UL (Unlimited Light).

Light-minded people are able to make things happen for themselves and are very clear on *who* they are, *what* they want, and *how* they want to connect to the people around them. When the change starts to happen inside of you, this is reflected not only in how you feel but by the impact you have upon the world. It is okay if you have dark moments, and even dark days when you buffer or log off; but try not to make it a consistent habit, and change your frequency back towards the light.

We are losing the war on mental well-being. We are living on the best version of the planet, but is humanity the best version of itself? It's time to manage your mind continuum and unlock your inner potential. We need to shift happiness to the forefront, and find solutions to allow people to stop searching and start to update differently.

Success is easy as it is based on time, but happiness is difficult as it's based on your mind. The reality is ultimately timeless, but your mind continuum is not. The greatest fight is within your own mind. Search every corner of your mind; keep looking for the solutions to discover your own frequency and make it consistent. Create hope for a better future for yourself and humanity, expect with confidence that an updated version is the new condition and have faith in something you cannot explicitly prove but you have complete trust in – these are all essential steps in the process of upgrading yourself to be better. Start becoming the human you were meant to be rather than what you were going to be. You are the only *you* in the world – you have one life but with many versions to update differently.

Happiness only occurs when you find the problems, you enjoy updating differently, and those solutions make a better you. Update differently and stop searching for happiness.

Update Ten
Be blinded by the light

T HE LIGHT MINDSET is a journey of self-development, but it's more about people coming out of the darkness and rethinking their situation to reach a higher level of achievement or find happier solutions.

As a fortieth birthday challenge, I used this model to support forty different people from a wide range of backgrounds and situations. I cannot use their names due to confidentiality, but I can share their journeys to show how they tried to update differently. I have named each one after a different colour as white light is the result of combining light of every colour.

1. **Apricot** is a young lady who is passionate about hair-dressing. She loves updating, but her dark mind creates a buffering process that causes anxiety and

stress to her mindset. She has a supportive environ-ment and is determined to succeed. Her own light solution was to care about herself by listening to music or going for a walk when she is having dark thoughts, and to make more pivotal decisions quickly, by just doing rather than over-planning.

2. **Bittersweet** is a mature lady who has been competent in her role for over 20 years; she feels undervalued and wants to exit the role, but fears the unknown and whether she can update for a new role. Her light solution was to create real bonds to give more love and attention to herself and her family, as there was an imbalance of energy invested in the workplace rather than the home.

3. **Blue-green** is a young man who is starting his journey of adulthood; he is juggling a business, a job and getting married too. Like many young entrepreneurs, he feels insecure and worried about having account-ability for his own decisions; he is also attached to the lifestyle and external value of brands. His light solution is to improve his self-confidence and believe in his own actions, and to disconnect from external factors and create real bonds by focusing on his own goals.

4. **Blue-violet** is a man who has experienced many dark moments in his life from death and divorce. His mind has been locked in a dark place for a very long time and is continuously buffering; he shuts down when it comes to any steps forward with new experiences. The only light in his life is his kids and his love for the

football team that he follows with passion. His light solution was to focus on self-development by reducing the buffering and taking small actions to update.

5. **Brick red** is a young man who fears believing in his passion of photography while doing a boring job. His dark mind is enjoying the feeling of external value as he is faking his own happiness. He continuously follows other people's lives and dreams, rather than focusing on his own. His light solution is to create real bonds to collaborate and communicate with others in his niche industry and follow the cues for success.

6. **Burnt sienna** is a young man who has just graduated from a university abroad; he has grown independently for over four years and is finding it difficult to adapt and fit in at home. He has developed a dark mind morning habit where he is buffering and not taking positive actions for the day ahead. His light solution is to remove the clutter and reduce the number of decisions that he makes in the morning so he can focus on the imbalance of the different updates.

7. **Carnation pink** is a young man who excelled in the education system and always aspired to the dream job with a top firm in London, which he achieved after university. He enjoyed it at first, but he struggled with his mental health and could not cope with the stresses of work. His light solution was to be active and fuel himself with the right food, and make time for developing stronger connections to the people that he cares for every day.

8. **Cornflower** is a mature man who is coping with the loss of his father. He is a highly driven and motivated individual, but he is finding it difficult to cope with looking ahead and supporting his mother with a different future. His light solution is to create a space where he and his mother can reflect and grow stronger together.

9. **Peach** is a highly intelligent vegan with soul and spirit who wants to become an entrepreneur, but everything in his environment has programmed him to be a worker. He wants to develop a business concept that would add value and change the world, but lacks self-confidence as he is taking the alternative path in his life. His light solution is to manage his time effectively and take positive actions to prepare for an uncertain future.

10. **Gold** is a university student who is finding himself and is looking for direction and purpose. He has issues making temporary bonds with people; he has disconnected with his old bonds and is reconnecting with new bonds, and is slowly growing his self-confidence and self-esteem.

11. **Grey** is a mature self-employed man who is very motivated but didn't really understand his own core values. Once he clarified his own core values he was able to align them with those of his business, as he realised that they were the same. The light solution was that he made his goals transparent and clear for him to focus on.

12. **Green-blue** is an aspiring music artist who is personally growing and producing content, but he lacks self-belief: not in his own content, but in the environment that surrounds him. His light solution is to focus on his own personal growth and be more resilient to the negative noise and feedback.

13. **Green-yellow** is a newly married man with two young babies, one being his daughter and the other, his business. He has good core values and, once he made a good plan, he was actioning and making progress every day. His light solution is to find the right imbalance between all the different updates and create positive bonds with his family and business through his own behaviours and actions.

14. **Lemon yellow** is a young girl who is very mature for her age and very driven in her studies. She lacks self-belief, and she shies away from social environments due to a lack of social skills. She is starting to create new bonds, and is developing strategies to connect with new people that will reduce anxiety and stress.

15. **Magenta** is trying to balance all the roles that he is currently working on but he has neglected his health and his well-being. His light solution is to create his own plan for a healthy lifestyle so he can be more active and discipline himself to make positive food and drink choices.

16. **Mahogany** is a modern mother who is managing a busy life while trying to develop a business idea. She is finding it hard to find time and energy for her new

business; but the real issue was self-esteem, as she did not doubt the business idea but doubted her own capability to run it.

17. **Maize** works from home and lives a busy life with his three kids. He is always buffering and finds it difficult to be reckless, as he sees the potential financial loss of every decision. Once he realised that his dark mind was at risk of being replicated in his kids, he quickly saw that he needed to change and update differently. I am so glad that he went MAD as it has impacted to make a happier home.

18. **Maroon** is an only child and has always worked from a young age. He is not happy in his current role at work and finds making decisions and taking actions extremely difficult. He has been programmed to be perfect and follow family rules and traditions, but he is slowly finding himself and developing the confidence to make better decisions for a lighter future. He has made the big decision to leave his job and look for a new direction.

19. **Melon** is a confident thirty-year-old party girl who is out every weekend, always searching for happiness. She has just changed jobs and I hope the different role will give her a new light in her life while creating new connections and bonds.

20. **Olive green** is a newly married man who realised that he was shining a light away from his key priorities, as he was following other people's dreams rather than